# My Port of Beirut

# My Port of Beirut

Lamia Ziadé

Translated by Emma Ramadan

PLUTO PRESS

First published by P.O.L éditeur as *Mon port de Beyrouth*, 2021
English language edition first published 2023 by Pluto Press
New Wing, Somerset House, Strand, London WC2R 1LA
and Pluto Press Inc.
1930 Village Center Circle, Ste. 3-834, Las Vegas, NV 89134

www.plutobooks.com

Cet ouvrage a bénéficié du soutien du Programme d'aide à la publication de l'Institut français

This book has been selected to receive financial assistance from English PEN's PEN Translates programme, supported by Arts Council England. English PEN exists to promote literature and our understanding of it, to uphold writers' freedoms around the world, to campaign against the persecution and imprisonment of writers for stating their views, and to promote the friendly co-operation of writers and the free exchange of ideas. www.englishpen.org

The translator would like to express her deep gratitude to the National Endowment for the Arts for its translation fellowship, as well as to Lamia Ziadé for her generosity and trust, and finally to her father, Mokhtar Ramadan, for his precious help and first-hand knowledge.

The right of Lamia Ziadé to be identified as the author of this work has been asserted in accordance with the Copyright, Designs and Patents Act 1988.

British Library Cataloguing in Publication Data
A catalogue record for this book is available from the British Library

ISBN 978 0 7453 4812 4    Paperback
ISBN 978 0 7453 4814 8    PDF
ISBN 978 0 7453 4813 1    EPUB

Typeset by Geraldine Hendler

Printed by Short Run Press, Exeter, Devon

*This book was written in the heat of the moment, with urgency, rage, and despair, in the four months that followed the explosion of August 4, 2020.*

# Contents

A message appears on my phone screen: "It's cursed, your poor country!" I imagine the friend who sent the message is referring to the terrible economic crisis that's had Lebanon plummeting to rock bottom for the last few months, and the Coronavirus pandemic that's been raging for a few days. As I'm about to set my phone back down, I notice that I also have seventy new messages on our family WhatsApp group, which has been somewhat inactive recently. Suddenly I have goosebumps. What's going on? The first of the seventy messages—"All safe?"—is sent by my cousin. My heart drops. Something bad has happened. With a pit in my stomach, I scroll through the next few messages. The first two—"yes" and "me too" sent one minute later by my brother and sister—confirm the urgency of the situation. The third, a photo of a sofa barely visible under the debris of a smashed patio door with the caption "I was sitting there a minute ago" is sent by one of my cousins, who is at the other end of the city, while another writes: "I don't have an apartment anymore." Then a selfie of my sister with her face bloodied, all the windows of her office shattered and the furniture in shambles, and my heart starts beating out of my chest. Immediately my mind goes to an Israeli bombing; it's been fifteen years now that they've been promising one, fifteen years that we've lived with their threats 24/7 and their planes flying over Lebanon several times a day for so many weeks. Trembling, I open the *L'Orient-Le Jour* website, but it's not loading. Then in the Whatsapp group, my brother shares a short video that was sent to him. The first images of the blast break me into a thousand pieces.

2

Despair, terror, anguish, devastation, distress. Since the explosion, I'm barely alive, I sob at all hours, I can't sleep at night, I go to bed in the early morning, I wake up two hours later thinking it was all a terrible nightmare, I realize a minute later that it wasn't a nightmare, it was real, I weep in my bed thinking of the destroyed silos. I am in Paris, but not for a single second do I think of anything other than Beirut. Beirut leveled, destroyed, traumatized.

I am riveted to my phone, toggling between WhatsApp and Instagram, because that's where everything is happening. Since the revolution that started in October 2019, it's the most efficient way to be informed. Everyone in Lebanon is their own press agency and updates come at the speed of light. Worse than the news are the images—terrible, unbearable. Apocalyptic images of the port and the city streets. And the videos of the explosion. Watched on a loop, watched in slow motion, ten, fifteen times per day.

I cry non-stop, like a five-year-old. I think of the victims, of the dead, of the wounded, mutilated, disfigured. Of those who lost their lives as they lost their homes. Of the houses, palaces, hospitals, all destroyed. Of all this tragedy that struck everyone simultaneously. Everyone in my family has had their apartments destroyed. My parents, my sisters, my brother, my aunts, my cousins. But—I hardly dare admit it—it's the pulverization of the port silos that affects me the most.

The silos were, for me, the most unshakable symbol of Beirut, barely scratched during the fifteen years of war, standing so tall, so white, in the prodigious light of the port, as majestic as snowy Mount Sannine towering over them in the distance.

As precious as the columns of Baalbek. They were our Egyptian pyramids. Nestled within the port, they were the identity of the city. Their constancy reassured me, their appearance comforted me, I thought of them as a pagan sanctuary that watched over the city. With the silos destroyed, anything was possible. Now there was nothing to stop Beirut from sinking into darkness.

*The front page on August 5, 2020.*

*The front page on July 12, 1982,*
*during the Israeli bombings of blockaded Beirut.*
*It's a curse, always in the summer.*

## 1

# The Sirens of the Port of Beirut

My grandmother's house, on rue Pasteur, has an unobstructed view of the Port of Beirut, right across from the silos, only a few hundred meters away. I spent most of my childhood Christmases in that house. Teta's pine tree, seven meters tall, touched the molding on the ceiling. The nativity scene, representing all of Judea, was at least three square meters, with an archaic but functioning water flow system symbolizing the River Jordan. The tree and the nativity scene were so magnificent that many family friends would bring their children to visit the last week of December, the way families go to peer in the windows of Galeries Lafayette in Paris.

At midnight on December 31, it was tradition for all the boats of the Port of Beirut to roar their sirens at the same time to ring in the new year. We would go out on the balcony for that magical moment. The sound was deafening and fantastic, the blaring announcement of a new year full of promise. And I would secretly make a wish, always the same: Please, God, let the war end this year.

During the restoration of our apartment, which had been struck by a Syrian firebomb during the attack on the Achrafieh neighborhood in 1978, my brother and I lived in that big house from another time, just a few hundred meters from the Green Line. Teta piled up two or three mattresses under her crystal Baccarat chandeliers in case a nearby explosive made them drop from the ceiling. Two bedrooms, a small living room and a bathroom, which were west-facing and in the firing line of a sniper, were off limits. It was in this house that my brother and I started our collection of shrapnel. We would gather shells after each bombing, on the little flat roof that we reached by climbing the rafters. Still today, I associate shrapnel with the smell of laundry, because on rainy days the clothes were hung to dry under the rafters, on lines strung between the beams. Kalashnikovs, bazookas, mortar shells, and other heavy weapons sometimes made holes in the walls, broke the windows, the tiles, and made the plaster on the ceiling crumble. At the end of the war, the house was damaged all over but still standing.

There is almost nothing left of that house after the August 4 explosion. The ceilings fell, the roof collapsed along with some of the walls, and most significantly, the facade with three finely crafted arches, its marble columns and its balcony with a view of the silos, no longer exists.

The photos that appear on my phone screen pierce my heart. I burst into tears thinking of my grandmother and sob for hours, inconsolable.

*A scene from a nightmare.*

One minute to midnight! Let's go out on the balcony
to listen to the port sirens! They'll keep away the city's
demons for the new year.

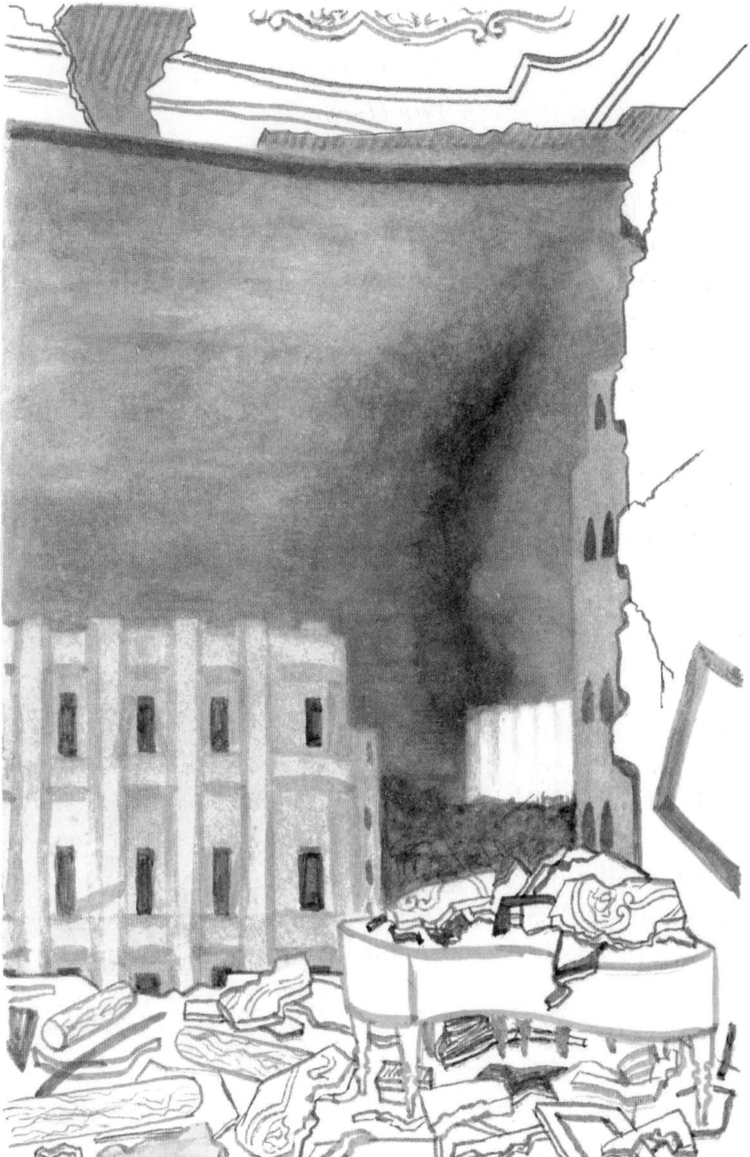

## 2

## *The Heroes*

The first face appears on my phone. A young, beautiful, beaming woman. She is sticking her smiling face through the open window of a firetruck. It's "the paramedic," my phone tells me, part of the brigade sent to the port at 5:54 p.m. to put out the fire in Hangar 12. Her name is Sahar Fares, she's twenty-seven years old, she died on Dock 9.

This face is seen around the world; within a few minutes it becomes the incarnation of the tragedy. Her body will be identified by her engagement ring. She was supposed to be married the following summer. Arriving at the port, she sent her fiancé a video of Hangar 12 in flames. That famous video is the only testimony of the final moments at the port. He called her, and as he was pleading with her to take shelter, the first explosion happened. Half a minute later, the second.

At her funeral, the orchestra booked for their wedding will play a zaffa, the traditional wedding song, and people will dance with her white casket. Just before, during the final goodbye at the Karantina fire station, her coworkers will wail the sirens from every firetruck at the same time to salute, in a deafening sob, "the bride of Beirut."

سحر فارس

"I am broken... life is meaningless now.
May God burn the hearts of those who robbed me of your smile and your
affection. You are my soul, and I will love you until I am reunited
with you once more...

...That rose, that child, strong as a hundred men, killed in an instant:
who can explain it to me..."

At the same time as this smile bursts through our screens, information on how the tragedy unfurled rapidly pours in and breaks our hearts: 2,750 tons of ammonium nitrate had been stored in Hangar 12 since 2013! The authorities knew it, even those at the very top. Including Aoun (I can't bring myself to call him the president), but we'll find that out later. A cache of fireworks had apparently been placed in the same hangar. The say the fire started around 5:50 p.m. In any event, at 5:54 p.m. the phone rings in the Karantina fire station. A brigade is sent to the port, including nine firefighters and one paramedic. They arrive at the site eight minutes later. They have no idea what's in the hangar.

A new photo appears on every phone. Three men, two firefighters and a civilian, try to force open Gate 11 of Hangar 12. The gate to hell. It's the last photo taken by Sahar and sent by WhatsApp to her fiancé a few seconds before the explosion. The nine men were between twenty and thirty-seven years old. Their faces invade the phone screens of the Lebanese people reeling from so much tragedy.

*Hell lies beyond this gate...*

جو بو صعب

*Joe Bou Saab and Ralph Mallahe had been best friends since childhood.*
*They are from Ain el Remmaneh.*

رالف ملاحي

*They joined the fire department together.*
*They were twenty-six and twenty-four years old.*

جو نون

*Joe Noun was twenty-seven years old*
*and from the village of Michmich.*

رامي كعكي

*Rami Kaaké had a four-year-old daughter.*
*He was the leader of the brigade.*

*The Beirut Fire Brigade.*
*Honor, sacrifice, devotion.*

شربل كرم

نجيب حتي        شربل حتي

*Nagib Hitti, Charbel Karam, and Charbel Hitti.*
*These three young men from the same family were inseparable.*
*They were from Qartaba, a village in the high peaks of Mount Lebanon.*
*Karlin, Charbel Hitti's sister, was married to Charbel Karam.*
*They have a two-year-old girl. Nagib Hitti was their cousin.*

مثال حوا

*Mithal Hawa was also engaged and planning to get married a few months later. At the very last minute, he offered to take the place of one of his friends for this mission.*

ايلي خزامي

*Elie Khouzami was the most senior of the brigade, having worked there since 2008. He was also supposed to be married soon.*

## 3

## "A steamer enters the haze of the Port of Beirut"

When we were on the balcony, my grandmother would often tell me how in the 1920s, the sea came right up to her house. The current port, built on the water, had not yet been constructed, and the Ottoman port, a bit farther to the west, consisted of a single basin and one seawall. I would daydream about it. About the old port, the steamers, the barges and the caiques that shuttled back and forth like a ballet between the docks and the ships. About the men in tarbooshes, the long women's traveling dresses, the heartrending goodbyes, the tragic voyages. I was crafting myself a novel.

I didn't know it then, but this incredible novel already existed. It's the story of Asmahan, born in 1917 on a boat between the Port of Izmir and the Port of Beirut and drowned in the Nile. I tell her story in my book *Ô nuit, ô mes yeux* whose very first page opens onto a drawing of the Port of Beirut at the beginning of the twentieth century. The first ten words of the book are: "A steamer enters the haze of the Port of Beirut." In the same book, I describe the arrival of Umm Kulthum at the Port of Beirut, coming from Alexandria in 1923. Ships greeted hers with ululations and ribbons, flags and flowers. A red carpet had been unfurled for her car, from the docks right up to the door of the Grand Théâtre. In my other books, *Bye Bye Babylon* and *Ma très grande mélancolie arabe*, I tell different stories of the port. The seizure of the free zone by the Phalangists at the very start of the war, and

*A drawing from* Ô nuit, Ô mes yeux.

the fires they set to cover up their crimes; the departure of the Palestinian soldiers and Yasser Arafat on the Atlantis, following the three-month blockade of Beirut and the siege of the city... No matter what happens, I always come back to the Port of Beirut. This port, its docks, its silos, its hangars, its cranes... my love, my passion. My obsession since August 4.

From the nineteenth century through the beginning of the twentieth, with the advent of photography, the visits of esteemed foreign boats were often commemorated with postcards. I have also photographed the Port of Beirut. Once in the 1980s, when I had just received a camera for Christmas, I was so excited to take black-and-white photos. Sailors posed for me with goats on the deck of a ship at the foot of the silos.

The second time was in 2010. For a few years, I had dreamed of returning to the port, but only those with the right authorization could enter. When by chance I mentioned this desire in front of a friend, he told that he owned, among other things, a lighterage company that someone else managed for him. He offered to arrange a visit of the port for me. The day arrived, but we couldn't drive there in his car, which didn't have the necessary permits. He asked an employee in charge of his on-site office to bring us instead. We drove around the port. Photos were strictly forbidden. I managed to take some photos from inside the car without anyone noticing, except the employee who shot me disapproving looks because he didn't want any trouble. I was fascinated by the gigantic cranes and the stacks of shipping containers, and by the incredible view of Beirut. I took a hundred photos that I haven't stopped looking at since.

*A drawing from* Bye Bye Babylon.
*The Port of Beirut was set on fire in April 1976,*
*after its famous free zone was pillaged.*
*The silos went unscathed.*

The most striking to me today, the ones that tie my stomach in knots, are the photos I took on Dock 9, between the silo and Hangar 12, my camera aimed at Beirut.

At the center of one of them is Lady Cochrane's villa, surrounded by yew trees, and just behind it, the top of the building where my parents have their apartment. Dizzingly close.

I dug out one of the numerous maps of Beirut stashed in my Paris apartment. It's been lying open on the ground for weeks. I measure the distances. My parents' apartment is 825 meters from Dock 9.

*Sailors posed for me with goats on the deck of a ship,*
*at the foot of the silos.*

*My photos of the port, taken in 2010.*

I took this photo at the very site of the explosion,
my camera aimed at Beirut. To the left, Hangar 12; to the right,
the silos. Behind the hangar is the top of the Electricité du Liban building
and, near the middle, the Saint Antoine church on rue Pasteur.

Another photo taken at the foot of the silos.

There, so close, Lady Cochrane's villa and its hundred-year-old yew trees.
Just behind, my parents' building.

## 4

## *The Sorcery of Objects*

There were thousands of books in my parents' apartment. In every room, piled up on the floor against every wall, since there was no more space on the shewlves, on tables, in boxes. Those books are the world I grew up in. Whenever I returned to my parents' house, I spent hours flipping through those unending rows looking for treasure. After the explosion, some of these books were found at the other end of the street, four or five buildings down. The rest of the apartment was also completely blasted away, like all the apartments in the neighborhood.

The photos of the devastation are very similar within a given perimeter. Patio doors torn from the walls, windows shattered, paintings thrown several meters from where they were hung, front doors dangling by their hinges, furniture upside down, and, in every home, a clock stopped at 6:07 p.m. In my parents' dining room, the heavy panels of the large cupboard containing the dishes flew to the other end of the room. Are you imagining the state of the dishes? Well, not a glass was cracked, not a single one moved even half a centimeter. The champagne coupes that were carefully aligned and balanced on top of each other are all intact. The opaline vase centerpiece on the living room table also did not budge one iota, while the dining chairs and armchairs that surrounded it lie overturned and broken a few meters away. The effects of the explosion are incomprehensible, corresponding to a mysterious and illogical system. Our neighbors' furniture was found 150 meters from the building... in the direction of the port! A sort of black magic appears to have organized the wreckage with wit and sophistication. My mother sends me a few photos of things as she found them.

These surprising still lifes are not exceptional. I know, because I've seen dozens of such photos on Instagram, that in every Beirut apartment the sorcery of objects was revealed. Sometimes, forgetting for half a second that my city is completely destroyed, I manage to smile at these haphazard assemblages.

*Among the debris, several epochs of the history of Lebanon.*

*This painting of eighteenth-century Beirut was*
*found several meters from where it was hung.*
*A piece of the canvas, just above the port, was ripped out.*
*It's the same shape and color as the explosion.*
*The sky had already been punctured by shrapnel in 1978.*
*My mother had had it restored at the end of the war.*

I do not have the same experience with the portraits of victims who will soon appear on my phone screen. They break my heart. Tears rapidly spring to my eyes. In all the photos sent around, their faces display magnificent smiles.

Since the 1970s, my father has obsessively collected newspapers
and magazines on the war in Lebanon. This issue of Time from 1982,
found by my mother on the kitchen floor, is not, however, from his stash, since
my father only reads the news in Arabic or in French. How many dozens of
meters did it travel to taunt us? Which of our neighbors has
also been archiving Lebanon's disasters?

*The first photos of the victims appear on phone screens,*
*with no names and no details. Just magnificent smiles.*
*Sometimes with members of their family.*

*Just magnificent smiles...*

*...happy expressions.*

*Then, gradually, names appear.*
*Delia Kedikian Papazian had two children.*

Alexandra Najjar was three years old.
She is one of the youngest victims of the explosion.
Photos of the little girl with her parents at the October protests and artist ren-
derings depicting her as an angel or with a flag will fill our phones.

*Ali and Malak Ayoub died together.*
*They had a little boy and a little girl.*

*Gaya Fodoulian was twenty-nine years old.*
*She died in her apartment in Achrafieh.*

*Jihad Saadé had just come back from Africa, where*
*he worked, to be with his little girl for her chemotherapy session.*
*He died in front of her eyes, in her room at the orthodox hospital.*

## 5

## *The Orthodox Hospital*

Immediately after the explosion, the wounded and their families head for the nearest hospitals. The Saint George Hospital, known in Beirut as "moustachfa el Roum," or as the "orthodox hospital," is the main one in the area. It's situated on the hill that directly overlooks the port, 750 meters as the crow flies from Hangar 12. Struggling on foot through the rubble and debris that blocks the streets, the wounded reach the doors of the hospital, but the hospital is destroyed. Pulverized. The hospitalized patients, the doctors, the nurses—all wounded. Some even dead. The tally will reach twelve patients, two visitors, and four nurses killed. The hospital won't fare any better than its neighbors. All the broken windows, the exploded walls, the fallen ceilings—but also, the smashed equipment. The incubators, the monitors... The testimonies of the wounded were recorded on video a few weeks after the explosion. It's difficult to find an account closer to a horror film than that of those mutilated women and men, blinded, mangled, bandaged, and stitched up, seated opposite the camera. They all describe the blast of the explosion as something monstrous, unlike anything they had ever felt before. They all believed they were about to die. They all, without exception, thought that the explosion had taken place in the hospital itself, in their unit, and that their colleagues in other units would come to their aid. Some believed it was a bombing directly on the hospital. That is actually a sentiment shared by everyone who was in

Beirut that day. Everyone within a two-kilometer radius of the port thought that the explosion was on their own street, in their own building. Another sensation felt by everyone who lived through that cataclysmic minute is the multiplicity of different perceptions experienced simultaneously. "If all the camera footage from the hospital had been gathered and each of us gave our testimony, we still would not be able to understand all the contradictory sensations felt at the moment of the explosion." "We are doctors, we know how to handle tragic situations, we are used to seeing the mortally wounded, we are trained in that. But what we experienced then is unlike anything else, it's indescribable, it crushed us all at the same time, and destroyed our equipment." "It was a slaughter; carnage in the patient rooms." "The special equipment was broken, and even the bandages and disinfectants were inaccessible because of the wreckage. There was a man with his skull cracked open, blood spilling everywhere, he was dying. I thought I could save him if I could stop the bleeding. My head and arm were wounded, some superhuman strength enabled me to lift the blown-off doors, step over the collapsed drop ceilings, and push aside the fallen walls to reach the closet where the strips of gauze and cotton were." "We intubated the wounded on the ground of the emergency room and stitched up others on the hood of a car." "Some used their ties to bandage wounds." "The elevators weren't working. We evacuated the patients from the ninth floor by the stairs, carrying them in sheets, or on pieces of drop ceiling, with a flashlight in our mouths because there was no electricity." "I felt a terrible pain in my chest, and my face was covered in blood.

I thought I was going to die, that the entire building had collapsed onto me. I couldn't move. A colleague from my unit dragged me out from under the rubble. We thought our colleagues from other units would arrive soon. We didn't imagine for a second that they were in the same boat. Once we had managed to leave our building, we saw the scope of the disaster and the influx of wounded people pouring in from the city. I had two broken ribs and a head wound, I was losing blood, but I had enough strength, positioning my phone in my mouth as a flashlight, to hastily stitch up several people on the sidewalk before I fainted."

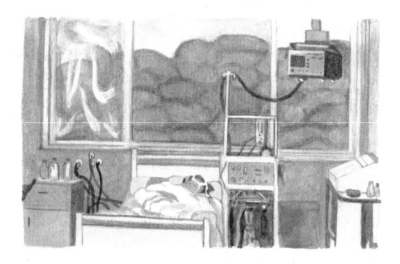

*The orthodox hospital in the 1980s.*
*Treatment continues behind sandbags.*

It's the first time in its history that the orthodox hospital, the oldest in Beirut, has ceased operating. During the fifteen years of war that ravaged Lebanon, it didn't stop for a single day, not even when the violent bombings came down on the neighborhood, striking some of its buildings directly. It was always rapidly repaired at the first lull, often financed by the USSR, an important source of aid for Greek Orthodox organizations during the war in the 1980s. I've been to the hospital on a few different occasions. That's where my two sisters were born. Sandbags were piled up outside the windows of the patients' rooms and the operating rooms, especially the windows facing west. I remember one day, in the early morning, when I walked between two rows of sick beds, lined up to the left and to the right of the hospital hallways, to reach the office of Dr. Fayez Bitar. The patients had been taken out of their rooms during the night because of a bombing. I had also spent the night in a hallway, the one in our apartment, screaming and writhing in agony because of a terrible stomachache, while the shells rained down outside. At the first ceasefire, my mother brought me to the hospital, convinced I had appendicitis. The night's wounded continued to flock there to the sound of ambulances. After examining me, Dr. Bitar told my mother, smiling, "She's fine, she was just very afraid." And suddenly I was also very ashamed.

That fear has never left me.

On August 4, the most seriously wounded are sent to other hospitals. But the three nearest hospitals have suffered as much damage as El Roum. The Karantina hospital is 900 meters from Hangar 12. It is essentially part of the port itself, in the zone where, in the nineteenth century, sick travelers who arrived at the Port of Beirut were quarantined. The Geitawi hospital, which is on the same hill as El Roum, is 1,200 meters from the hangar. The Rosary Sisters Hospital in Wardieh, on rue Pasteur, adjoins my grandmother's house, and so is 650 meters from Hangar 12. Today everyone in Beirut knows the exact number of meters that separated them from the grain silos on August 4, 2020, at exactly 6:07 p.m.

*The reception desk at the Hôtel–Dieu,*
*one of the few hospitals spared by the explosion.*

*At the orthodox hospital, a baby is*
*born at the exact moment of the blast.*

*This photo taken by a press photographer was seen around the world.*
*Young nurse Pamela Zeinoun, after managing to extract herself from the debris,*
*removes three premature babies from their broken incubators. The entrance to*
*the maternity ward, as well as the emergency exit, are blocked by rubble, but*
*she manages to carry them outside, where she discovers a horrific scene in the*
*parking lot: the ground is strewn with the dead and wounded. She decides to go*
*to the nearest hospital to find them an incubator. With the babies in her arms,*
*she walks for forty-five minutes. The neighboring hospitals are destroyed and*
*cannot help her. On the highway, she stops a car that brings her to the mater-*
*nity ward in Zalka, in the north of Beirut. The babies are saved. In this photo,*
*she is at the welcome desk at the orthodox hospital, where, before leaving,*
*she calls her mother to let her know she's alive.*

Doctors and nurses sit one after another in front of the camera to give their testimonies. "What I first heard, felt, was an earthquake. The monstrous explosion didn't come until later."

The testimony of Dr. Nadine Massaad:
"We climbed into the ambulance. We drove at full speed, but also terrifyingly slowly, the streets were completely jammed... I felt time slipping away... I was taking care of her, but I also had to be mindful of the other wounded... I was mainly focused on her... such a little girl, and her situation was critical... I was still in a state of indescribable shock... I cared for her throughout the entire journey... her father was consumed with anxiety for his daughter, but at the same time he helped me contact my parents to reassure them, to tell them that I was alive... He took my phone and asked for their number"—the young woman breaks off for a few seconds, choked with sobs—"so that I could speak to them... and I said to him: It's going to be okay, Alexandra will be alright, I'm going to do everything I can to get Alexandra to the nearest hospital..."

## 6

# *Lady Cochrane*

For Lady Cochrane's legendary "villa," also known as Sursock Palace, the number is 750. Just 750 meters separate the most beautiful palace of Beirut from Hangar 12; 750 meters without a single small obstacle, with the exception perhaps of the branches of a few yew trees, palm trees, magnolias, or jacarandas in the vast garden surrounding the villa. The explosion blast encountered nothing on its journey between the hangar and the villa that could mitigate it even slightly; the destruction is total. By smashing to pieces that architectural and artistic splendor, the explosion not only demolished the most beautiful palace in Beirut and the exceptional works of art it housed, but also the most glorious symbol of resistance to the two plagues that have blighted the city over the course of the past decades: the war, and real estate development. The woman who made it into such a symbol, through her willpower and determination, is Lady Yvonne Sursock Cochrane, heiress to one of the most esteemed Greek Orthodox families in Lebanon. The Sursocks fled the sack of Constantinople in 1453 and controlled a real estate, agricultural, and industrial empire in Egypt, Palestine, Syria, and Lebanon, where they chose to settle on that hill overlooking the sea. Daughter of Alfred Bey Sursock, the Consul General of the Ottoman Empire in Paris, and Donna Maria Teresa Serra di Cassano, of Neapolitan high society, Yvonne Sursock married an Irish Lord.

*Yvonne Sursock Cochrane on*
*her birthday in 2019.*

Refusing to leave the palace throughout the fifteen years of war, even during the deadliest battles, Lady Cochrane tirelessly repaired the damage inflicted by the various clashes, and it took twenty years of additional work to restore it to the jewel it had once been. After the war, she was fiercely opposed to the reconstruction of Beirut as envisioned by Rafic Hariri and fought against the savage real estate development that disfigured the city. In the 1960s, she founded the Association for Protecting Natural Sites and Old Buildings, of which she remained president for many years. She described the architecture of Lebanese houses as being unique for its exquisite gracefulness. The blast of the explosion blew it all away in a second. A single second that caused more damage than fifteen years of war. Italian marble statues, stucco, woodwork, and stained-glass windows from Maison Tarazi, Persian rugs, Flemish tapestries, paintings by masters, family portraits, a Neapolitan entrance gate, rugs woven in Smyrna, leather wall panels, crystal chandeliers from Bohemia, Russian icons, busts from Palmyra—all in pieces, in tatters, in shreds.

But the tragedy doesn't end there. The losses are not only material or symbolic. Yvonne Cochrane was having tea in her living room overlooking the Port of Beirut on August 4, at 6:07 p.m. The explosion blast flung her several meters away. She died as a result of her injuries. At the funeral, her daughter removed the wreath sent by the Presidency of the Republic that had been placed on her casket.

*The sorcery of objects once more.*

*At the palace entrance, the broken pilaster had been left there in memory of the destruction of the war of 1975. Who could have imagined that one day things would be far worse?*

*Portrait of Lady Cochrane on the palace terrace in 1951.*
*The third port basin did not yet exist.*

*The view today. Between the yew trees, the silos.*
*Behind the photographer, the devastated palace,*
*but the planters on the terrace have not budged.*

*The palace is in the same state as this Chinese vase.*

*These pieces of broken porcelain were photographed by Gregory Buchakjian, a longtime archivist of the ruins of Beirut. Many similar photos will be shared during those weeks of August.*

7

## The Third Basin

The former Ottoman port, constructed by a Frenchman, the Comte de Perthuis, was located farther west, at the very site of the ancient port of Phoenician in Greco-Roman times. When the famous school of law was founded in Beirut in the second century, welcoming students from Arabia, Persia, and also Europe, the port had to be fortified. This school trained the most important legal experts and people claimed "peace will not extend throughout the world until we follow the laws of the school of Beirut." In the nineteenth century, as a result of the significant activity spurred by the founding of the American and Jesuit universities in the city, the Ottomans called on the Comte to construct the port, as well as the Beirut-Damascus highway. The port was later modernized and equipped with a second basin in the 1930s, under the French mandate.

"Henry's the one who built the port," my grandmother would tell me sometimes, on her balcony, nostalgic. By the port, my grandmother meant the most recent and vastest part, which was built in the 1960s. By Henry, she meant the Executive Council of Major Projects, of which Henry was one of the most eminent leaders. Henry was the husband of Aunt Marcelle, my grandmother's sister. In our family he enjoys immense prestige and a particular affection, not only because he was assassinated in the first year of the war. He was an extraordinary person, brilliant and free.

64

In the mid-1960s, Lebanon's president, Fouad Chehab, decided to build a third basin in the Port of Beirut. Wanting Lebanon to have modern infrastructure and controlled urban development, he created the Executive Council for Major Projects a few years prior, appointing the most competent men in their fields. Henry Naccache, one of the first Lebanese to earn a degree from the École Polytechnique in Paris and an engineering degree from École des Mines, is one of the most senior members of this department. He directed the construction of the Beirut airport, the Lebanese University, electrical installation in the villages, the road network, the Litany River Dam, the Central Bank, and many other projects that uplifted the country. He also proposed to the president, who acquiesced, that the International Fair in Tripoli be entrusted to the Brazilian architect, Oscar Niemeyer. (When he comes to spend a month in Lebanon in 1962, Nïemeyer, who is afraid of flying, will disembark at the Port of Beirut.) One of the large-scale projects he will undertake in 1963 is indeed the construction of the third basin of the Port of Beirut and its grain silos; 60 million Lebanese lira are set aside for the project. Once the task is complete, Henry asks the President of the Republic for a favor: he has saved 15 million of the budget allocated for the construction of the basin. He would like permission to use these funds for the development of a yacht club in Jounieh. The small Beirut yacht club had been located where the third basin was constructed, and it would be beneficial, for the prestige of the country, for Lebanon to have a yacht club worthy of its name. Chehab grants his permission.

*The construction and painting of the silos. Photo taken from the second basin.*

This story about the budget amazes me. I have trouble imagining today that there were once men in Lebanon who didn't do absolutely everything to take advantage of their government position to pillage the country and fill their own pockets. It seems inconceivable. A budget not stolen, not diverted, not even surpassed, not even spent, but saved for other infrastructure projects. Those men (under Fouad Chehab's rule, Henry was not the only one) strove to turn Lebanon into a nation. Henry often had to battle to execute projects he was in charge of, without succumbing to the pressures of traditional political leaders. Those who wanted to modify the route of a highway so that it passed through their village, or the path of a road so that it ran alongside their villa. And these are only the most innocuous examples... Fouad Chehab himself had to fight all throughout his presidency against powerful feudal leaders in order to follow through on his vision for a democratic Lebanon, one that would be rigorous and socially-minded. But things will change. At the end of his term, Fouad Chehab declines to amend the constitution so that he can be reelected. Six years later, after the pathetic mandate of his successor, he is solicited to run in the presidential election. He gives a speech that has since become historic: he declares that the numerous contacts he has established and the analysis he has conducted have convinced him that Lebanese politicians—whom in private he calls *"fromagistes"* or "cheese-eaters" because of their embezzlement/misappropriation of funds—are not prepared to abandon traditional feudal politics and a monopolistic economy to establish a modern and socially responsible state. He ends his speech by announcing that, for this reason, he will not run in the election. Lebanon is henceforth delivered to those who will lead it to its ruin. This communiqué is released on August 4, 1970. Fifty years to the day before the blast.

*Guaranteed a parliamentary majority for his election,*
*President Chehab releases a communiqué stating his refusal to run.*
*In concise and severe terms, he puts the political mores*
*of the time on trial.*

Suleiman Frangieh is elected President of the Republic by one vote, during a Parliament election that concludes under threat of violence. It's the beginning of Lebanon's demise. And the beginning of problems for Henry, who refuses to congratulate the new president. His friends insist. Not only does he not go, but he makes it known, proclaiming in salons: "I will not go congratulate that gangster." Because Frangieh is a godfather, handed the presidency by the most important feudal leaders from each Lebanese community. These leaders want a president who will stop the democratic reforms begun by Chehab and maintain the feudal system that keeps power in their hands. These bitter political enemies are all in agreement for once and unite to put Frangieh in power. Henry's hostility evidently gets back to Frangieh.

Twelve years earlier, in a church in the village of Miziara, in his North Lebanon fiefdom, Suleiman Frangieh took part in a shootout against a rival clan family that resulted in twenty-one deaths. With a warrant out for his arrest, he took refuge in Syria, where he befriended a young officer by the name of Hafez al-Assad. Pardoned eighteen months later, he returned to Lebanon. The day of the election, at the end of August 1970, he arrives at Parliament with a few hundred armed supporters who wait at Place de l'Étoile. According to Jonathan Randal, the famous *Washington Post* correspondent, what came next was like a western: In the third round of voting, Frangieh beats the Chehabist candidate by one vote. Outside, his supporters shoot into the air, thinking their candidate has been elected. The Speaker of Parliament announces that there must be a fourth round, since neither of the two candidates has a clear majority. Frangieh, who is armed, rushes toward him, yelling: "*I won't let myself be cheated like this!*" Five of his men, brought into the assembly hall with a gendarme on their side, aim their weapons at him. There will be no fourth round; Frangieh is declared president.

One month after Suleiman Frangieh's inauguration, Henry is accused by the new Prime Minister, Saeb Salam, of corruption, of stealing funds meant for one of his projects, and he is fired from the council. Saeb Salam, leader of an

*President Fouad Chehab*

important feudal family in Beirut, is a longstanding adversary of Chehab and a bitter rival of his own brother Malek Salam, then president of the Executive Council for Major Projects, who is also fired based on this same accusation of corruption. In reality it was a familial and political vendetta. The accusations are unfounded, no proof is offered. Malek Salam and Henry Naccache take legal action which will exonerate them from the false charges brought against them. In the meantime, both are distanced from the Council. Henry will have numerous offers for

*Henry Naccache at his desk at the Executive Council for Major Projects.*

prestigious positions in the private sector, for banks. He will turn down all of them to pursue studies in biology, saying, "I am not on this Earth to make money!" A few years later, his *Essay on the Dynamic Laws of Evolution*, based on mathematical modeling, is about to be published when the war breaks out.

A true Francophile, he thinks about moving to France during the first years of the war. He spends time there in the fall of 1975 with Aunt Marcelle but quickly decides that his country, the country he loves, is Lebanon, that his place is in the Kara building, rue Zarif, and they return to Beirut.

*Henry at the beginning of the 1970s.*
*I always saw this photo in a frame at Aunt Marcelle's house*
*in Maad, where she lived for the rest of the war.*

Faithful to his vision of a multi-confessional Lebanon, he refuses to leave his majority Muslim neighborhood to move to the "Christian ghetto." When the public high school in Zarif struggles to cover courses in 1976, Henry volunteers as a chemistry teacher.

He will teach a few classes before he is assassinated. He was supposedly killed by "rogue individuals" at a "flying checkpoint." Back then, in both camps, citizens were killed at random based on their religion, which was marked on their identity card. That's what I always believed happened to Henry.

Today, suddenly, I can't help but see things differently. The violence of the August 4 explosion shook up all my certitudes and cast a new, blinding light onto our past. Was Henry killed at random? At random, a man like him? Would Lebanon rid itself at random of all its men of great value, giving free rein to incompetent men and crooks? Did chance empty the country of those men? Killed or forced into exile, or into fear and silence. Chance? Luck, destiny, fate? Maybe it's true, maybe not. And even if it is true, in reality, it's false.

A hazy and insidious process was begun in 1970, by a handful of men with no vision and no scruples, determined to preserve their privilege, power, and money, by placing at the head of government a mobster, the embodiment of feudalism and corruption, who, day after day, after day, after day, led Lebanon to the gates of hell. Several times to the gates of hell, and after fifteen years of war this mechanism that consists of removing, at every echelon, the most competent and upstanding men, the nuisances, for the profit of incapable corrupt men, is still the same today. That explosion, the most monstrous anyone could ever imagine, which destroyed the third basin constructed by Henry, and Beirut, and the Lebanese, is a legacy of the vultures of the 1970s: Camille Chamoun, Kamal Joumblat, Saeb Salam,

*The final second of the world from before.*

Pierre Gemayel, Kamel Assaad, Rachid Karami, and many others. Some of these family names are the same as those of our present-day criminals.

I have just learned something that gives me goosebumps. When will this curse end? Ten words appear on my phone: "Suleiman Frangieh is running for President of the Republic." It's the grandson of Suleiman Frangieh, the president elected in 1970.

*Henry on the land where the Beirut airport will be constructed
in the 1940s, another of his major projects.*

*Jessica Kahwaji Daoud, a nurse, died*
*on the ninth floor of the orthodox hospital.*
*She had two children.*

*Lina Bou Hamdan, another nurse who died
at the orthodox hospital.*

*The young nurse Jessica Bezdjian*
*also died at the orthodox hospital.*

*Amer Hussein, a Syrian sailor, was
working on a boat at the time of the explosion.
He was twenty-five and engaged to be married.*

*Amin Zahed was found at sea thirty hours after the explosion.*
*He was the father of two children.*

*Mireille Germanos, another nurse who died at the orthodox hospital.*

## 8

## My Sister's Friends

It's one in the morning, my phone rings. It's my sister calling from Lebanon: One in the morning, which means two in Beirut. My heart skips a beat. I can't feel my legs beneath me. These late phone calls from Lebanon, for the past few years now, scare me. Just before picking up, I always dread the announcement of more bad news. Since August 4, it's been even worse. I've already spoken to my sister twice today... I prepare myself for a catastrophe. But my sister simply wants to talk, she knows I go to sleep late, didn't think she would be disturbing me. She's just come back from dinner at the home of friends of friends who live in the region where our family has a house and where she's taken refuge. It's the first time she's gone out since the explosion, more than a month and a half ago. She needed to take her mind off of things. Since August 4, she has nightmares every night. More or less the same nightmare. She dreams that the house is crumbling on top of her, stands up and runs out of her bedroom before realizing that the house is not in fact crumbling. Suffocating and drenched with sweat, she gathers herself, splashes her face with water in the bathroom, then goes back to bed. And her nightmare picks up right where it left off. On and on, night after night.

She tells me about the dinner. She was not able to take her mind off of things. "I ate at Nidale and Ghassan's... Two friends I barely know. They suggested I come over because one of our mutual friends is staying with them for a few days. Their best friend, Chant, died in the explosion."

That day, Nidale was high up in the mountains, about fifty kilometers from Beirut, with Chant's wife, Nairy, when they heard the explosion. The blast was so powerful that they thought it happened in Faraya, the neighboring ski resort. Nairy immediately sent a message to her husband to reassure him, to tell him that she and the children were fine. When the two women realized what had actually happened, Nairy tried to reach Chant but wasn't able to.

Two other guys from the same group came to dinner. Julien and Ronald. Ronald lives primarily in Saudi Arabia, but his wife, Charly, lives in Beirut, in Skyline, the Bernard Khoury building. They were just married, right before the Coronavirus pandemic broke out, and each found themselves stuck in a different country. Charly filmed the fire from her window and sent the video to Ronald and Julien. Julien, who lives in Sama Beirut, Lebanon's tallest tower, opened his window to film it too. And so, at the moment of the explosion, he was not pulverized with glass. He was simply thrown several meters. He was not wounded. Charly saved Julien.

Ronald, from Saudi Arabia, hears the explosion on his phone while telling Charly to move away from the window. He tries to call her back with no luck. At one point she picks up but doesn't speak, her Apple Watch probably answered on its own. Ronald calls his father, who lives in Hazmieh, and tells him: "I'm worried Charly is dead. Go see what's going on." Then he calls Julien, whom Nairy has also called to ask to go check on her husband. He says: "Once you've checked on Chant, go see Charly." He didn't want to ask him to prioritize Charly over Chant. Julien takes his motorcycle and heads for Gemmayzeh at full speed. It's an apocalyptic spectacle. He drives over a carpet of glass that squeaks along the streets strewn with the dead and wounded. Ronald's father gets as close as he can to the Skyline building in his car, then abandons it and walks the rest of the way.

Julien enters the East Village building to look for Chant. He doesn't find him at home. He checks for his car in the parking lot. He tells himself that he must have left on foot or been carried by someone. He stops by Jean-Marc's apartment, glances quickly through the smashed door, sees no one and continues on to Charly's house. Later he will feel guilty because he might have saved Jean-Marc if he had entered.

He runs to Charly's. Ronald's father is in the apartment. He tells him that she's not there. In fact, she was under the debris, at their feet, arms broken, stomach ripped open, her liver nearly hanging out. With the help of a strong neighbor, they wrap her in a curtain and place her on an armchair so that they can carry her, and go down the stairs. They try to put her on the motorcycle but can't manage to keep her upright because she's completely shattered. They carry her and run to the highway where they try to stop one of the many ambulances passing by. Two ambulances stop, but they have no room. Each is carrying six or seven wounded. They stop an old Honda that takes them. Knowing it will be difficult to find a hospital in Beirut, they head for Zalka. Meanwhile, Ronald tries to reserve a room in the hospital from Saudi Arabia. As if anyone could still reserve anything at all...

At the Zalka hospital, the wounded litter the ground. A nurse in tears tells them that if they want to have a chance at saving her, they have to find another hospital. The driver of the Honda thinks of Bellevue hospital, where he knows someone. They turn around and drive the wrong way down the highway, back in the other direction, towards Mansourieh.

They arrive at the Bellevue hospital. The doctors place her in intensive care. Her two arms have suffered a complicated fracture that requires external rods that are rarely available. Fortunately they have them. If not, they would have had to amputate. Her liver is also barely saved. A single blood vessel remains unsevered. One of her eyes is damaged.

Meanwhile, Julien has returned to look for Chant with Ghassan. They find him on the roof of the building where he had gone to film the fire, along with the concierge and a friend, Ray. Ray had gone up to the roof and then rushed back down in a panic to his apartment to check on his wife and children. The children are okay, his wife gravely wounded. Her face is completely ripped open and gushing blood. He brings her outside with the help of a friend, Max. A car stopped and brought them to Hôtel-Dieu. The children saw everything, they're traumatized. The concierge is dead.

Julien and Ghassan find Chant. Despite his size, they manage to get him downstairs. They bring him to the hospital. I don't know how they manage to get him to Hôtel-Dieu. The doctors try to revive him but don't succeed. Like in the movies, they announce the hour of death in front of the two friends and write his name on a Post-it. They spell it wrong, because his name is complicated, it's Armenian. There are no more stretchers available. Ghassan finds himself pushing his friend again in a cart to the morgue and Julien returns to Bellevue to see Charly. There is no more room at the morgue, the cadavers are lined up on the ground and labelled with Post-its.

Chant's phone continued to film after the blast. You can hear his voice in the video for a few seconds, then the battery runs out...

Charly spends weeks in the hospital and undergoes several operations, then is finally released. She cannot move her arms at all but begins physical therapy. She has still not regained sight in her eye. Several months later, she continues to find tiny pieces of glass in her hair, her ears... She asks every day for news about her hospital roommate. They tell her that she was released and is doing well, but in reality no one knows...

Chant's children ask their mother: "Do you think Papa is eating well, where he is?"

Nairy cannot bear for her husband to be seen as a victim. He will remain a hero in her eyes, and in the eyes of her children.

*A new photo of the fire brigade makes the rounds on everyone's phones.*
*Apparently it was taken on their way to the port.*

*Asmahan Sarrouf Bou Rjeily was in her house in Gemmayzeh with
her husband and daughter at the time of the explosion.
Her husband and the six-year-old girl were wounded but survived.*

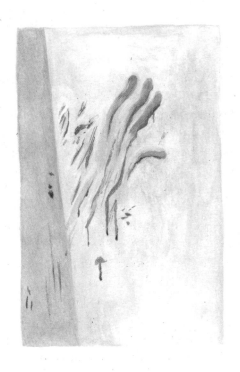

*A new type of photo appears on Instagram:*
*smears of blood on the walls.*

9

## *Guilt*

Hanging up the phone, I feel guilty. I'm angry at myself for not returning to Beirut immediately after August 4, to support, shoulder, surround those who are there, bruised and traumatized. My family, my parents, my sisters, my brother, my nephews, my cousins, but not just them. My country. I know well, however, the terrible collective feeling of abandon they must feel, for having experienced it myself—along with every Lebanese—during the war. I remember my father furious in front of the TV screen, when we managed to get the French channels and see the eight o'clock news and it began with the announcement of Giresse's tragically sprained ankle or Noah's elimination in the semifinals of Roland-Garros, while we had just spent our third consecutive night in a shelter. "*Faziʒin!* [These journalists] are unbelievable! Beirut is burning, we're being massacred like rats, and all the world cares about is sports." Today, the Lebanese still living in the country fear that, once the initial global outrage has passed, some humanitarian aid provided, the fate of Lebanon will no longer interest anyone. The mass departure of Lebanese people who are able to leave exacerbates this feeling of isolation. "We find ourselves alone again," my sister says to me, "all our friends are going abroad, our children's friends too." And I feel guilty. I had planned to spend a month in Beirut in September, and I canceled. I canceled because I'm AFRAID. Not being able to enjoy the easy life in Lebanon, the nightlife, the beaches, the restaurants, I don't care about any of that. Beirut plunged into darkness, morose Beirut, destroyed Beirut, I can tolerate that perfectly well, I know that Beirut. I love that Beirut. The difficulty of daily life, the shortages, the lack of electricity and water, I can go back to that without a problem. What I cannot bear to relive is the fear. I am no longer capable of it. The fear of dying. I'm a total coward, I can't help it... In reality, it's the return itself that I fear, the trip to Beirut. The journey from Paris to Beirut is beyond my abilities. I have too many memories...

In 1989, I had been studying in Paris for two years. During every school vacation—All Saints' Day, Christmas, February break, Easter, and summer—I went back to a Lebanon at war. Today, that seems insane to me. At the time, it seemed perfectly normal to go back to my country and my family as soon as no other obligation kept me abroad. This sentiment must have been largely inspired by my parents, who never wanted to leave Lebanon, even in its worst moments.

August 5 or 6, 1989, I take the plane from Paris to Cyprus, then a ferry, the *Santa Maria*, to the port of Jounieh, at night. In recent weeks, the situation in Lebanon has gone up in flames. Savage bombings of several regions and residential neighborhoods in Beirut, violent clashes on numerous fronts. People flee by sea, by the tens of thousands, while the airport is closed. Arriving in Lebanese waters, the boat turned off all its lights, so as not to be spotted. We plunge into the black night. Into the black sea. Then the Lebanese coast appears in the distance, obscure. The mountains. Then we can see the bombings. The flash of rapid lights, explosions. I am terrified at the idea of what awaits us. They tell me not to worry, that the bombings target the coastline between Beirut and Jounieh, but that in Jounieh we'll be okay. We touch land. We disembark in a hurry. Suddenly the port of Jounieh is struck by Syrian artillery. The ferry quickly retreats from the shore, without unloading the bags, but with the passengers leaving for Cyprus on board. The fishing port building, where we take shelter, is a single story. Not reassuring in the least. They tell us to get flat on our stomachs with our hands over our heads. I remember finding that ridiculous, but I throw myself to the ground anyway, trembling. I am terrified. In my memory, the bombing lasts about ten minutes. It might have been shorter, but it felt endless to me. I truly believed that I was going to die. When it stops, we come running out of the building. I find my father, who is waiting for me outside, sheltered under a sort of covered courtyard, and we drive in record time to the mountain where my mother is being eaten alive with worry. The next day, we learn on the radio that two small girls, sisters, drowned in the bay of Jounieh during the bombing, right in front of their parents. They were among the passengers taking the ferry in the other direction, fleeing the hell of Lebanon. That night, dozens of other people died throughout the country. A funereal night. One of my mother's best friends, Mouna, died in her magnificent house in Beirut, which she refused to leave. I am rattled by this new atrocity that has struck someone I know so intimately.

*The day after my return, the front page of* L'Orient-Le Jour:
*"Lebanon Hurtles off a Fatal Cliff*
*Sheer Terror Every Weekend Night*
*Massacre in a Shelter in Fayadieh*
*Two Children Killed at Sea in Jounieh."*

*At the funeral for their two young daughters.*

The authorities of the Port of Jounieh contact me two days later: my suitcase, which fell into the sea the night of my return, like that of many passengers going between Jounieh and Cyprus, like the little girls Ruba and Maya, has been fished out of the water. I had forgotten about it, I had thought of only one thing since that night: "I am alive." It was filled with a stash of novels, in preparation for the long days of not being able to leave the house. The books, gorged with water, had quintupled in size. I dried them in the sun. I still grab them from my library sometimes and give them a lick. They taste like salt.

August 15, 2013, I am on the Air France flight from Paris to Beirut with my two children. I am slightly tense, as usual, although that year there's no reason to be. One fourth of a Lexomil helps me pass the four-hour flight, which I follow closely on the screen in front of me. Not long before we arrive at the Lebanese coast, I am already pleased, we are on the left side of the plane and can glimpse the coast of Beirut, a sight that floods me with joy. But, on my screen, I watch the plane turn and head for inland Lebanon instead of flying along the coastline toward the airport. I am startled and suddenly very worried. My children groan: "Stop trying to give us your anxiety." But I know it's not normal; now we're flying over Beqaa. Everyone on the plane is asleep or watching a movie. The lights have been off for hours. I ask a flight attendant walking down the aisle where we're going. She bursts into tears and answers: "To Amman, madame." This alerts the other passengers, questions fly, but the attendant leaves in a hurry, saying she doesn't know anything more. Then we realize that the pilot hasn't made any announcements for over an hour. Panic. The word Amman is so closely associated in my mind with the diverting of planes, because of Black September, that I am already imagining the worst. On my screen, we are suddenly over Damascus. Then we circle over Damascus. We are certainly not going to Amman. Finally, the captain announces that we are about to land, with no further explanation. In 2013, we are already in the middle of the Syrian war. Hysteria in the cabin. My daughter's teeth chatter in a way I've never seen before except in cartoons. She is terrified. I give her an entire Lexomil. We land with no lights on. A dark runway. As soon as we're on the ground, the captain asks us to lower our window shades, but we have time, just before, to see armed men in military vehicles surrounding the plane, their weapons pointed at us. My son takes out his phone and calls his father. He tells him we landed in Damascus. "I wanted to tell you that I love you, Papa." We are all convinced that we've been taken hostage and that we might not make it out alive. Some cry, others pray. We learn that the ambassador of France as well as three Lebanese deputies are in first class. Then, about an hour of fear later, we finally take off again. We will spend the night in Cyprus before leaving for Beirut the next day.

We never found out what really happened. The official version: imaginary issues on the road to the airport in Beirut, so Air France decided it was better not to land there, but instead divert to Amman (even though the Larnaca airport in Cyprus is closer). On the way, the captain realized that he didn't have enough fuel to reach Amman, so he decided to land in Damascus—why not? In the same half hour, another Air France plane coming from Nice, as well as a British Airways plane, both landed in Beirut, apparently without any concerns for what was happening on the road to the airport. The official version convinces no one. But the result is the same, the fear remains. The fear that on my next trip to Lebanon, something will go wrong...

I return to my phone: I was never on social media before, but for the last year I've been spending all my time on Instagram, since October 2019. What horrible news will pop up to make my stomach churn this time? What face will break my heart? Some clichés are posted and reposted endlessly. The collective sadness of the Lebanese people is transmitted through these images that everyone has seen a hundred times, and which, even the hundredth time, evoke tears. The photos of their smiles, or their funerals.

*Elias Khoury, fifteen years old. And that smile...*

*Carried by his high school friends.*
*The Lebanese people are devastated by so much misfortune.*

*The Lebanese people cannot handle any more,*
*they are broken, anguished, desperate.*
*Even those who haven't lost a loved one, or their home...*

*...have no more tears left to cry.*

*Sahar's selfie becomes iconic.*

*A video of Marine Najem, another victim of the explosion, was filmed by her granddaughter a few months prior. We see the grandmother, very chic, joyously chanting "thawra, thawra," as her grandchildren prepare to join the protests in Martyrs' Square.*

# 10

## *Sacy and Noun*

The days pass, but the sadness, the anguish, the despair, do not. Each day the news is worse than the day before, the extent of the disaster continues to reveal itself. On our phone screens, terrible personal accounts of August 4 are told in great detail, they lacerate our hearts. New photos of destroyed buildings make me rage; those of disfigured or mutilated people make me cry. A report from inside the Beirut hospitals devastates me. The images are horrific.

Those taken of the explosion from the inside by surveillance cameras give a sense of the apocalyptic scene experienced by the staff and patients. There are no words. Images of destruction, of debris everywhere, mountains of rubble, crumbled facades, collapsed ceilings, high-tech equipment reduced to scrap metal. There are also images of children in the pediatric oncology unit of the orthodox hospital. This unit, on the ninth floor with a panoramic view of the port, was blasted with extraordinary violence. The children there on August 4 at 6:07 p.m., on top of the trauma of their cancer and their chemotherapy, must also endure that of the explosion and must heal from serious physical injuries. This little girl in the arms of her mother was not wounded, by some miracle. She was happy to have her father with her that day for her chemo session. He had come back from Africa, where he works, just to be at her side. He died right in front of her, in her hospital bed, at 6:08 p.m. that Tuesday. There are other terrible images.

The butterflies, blooming trees, birds, fruits, clouds, red mushrooms with white spots surging gaily from the vestiges of the Karantina hospital, which housed six intensive neonatal care units available free of cost to those most in need—now nothing but a field of ruins. Unlike the orthodox hospital, it was ground-floor only, and is now open-air...

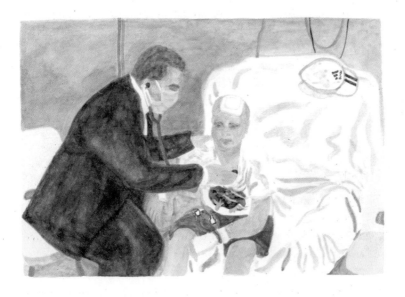

*Dr. Noun visits one of his youngest chemotherapy patients at*
*the orthodox hospital, relocated to a hospital in Byblos after August 4.*
*The young boy suffered a head wound.*

But far worse than the images are the testimonies. That of Peter Noun, a doctor in the pediatric oncology unit of the orthodox hospital. And that of Robert Sacy, whom I know well because he had been my youngest sister's pediatrician during the war and is still the pediatrician of my nephews to this day. He is the one who created the pediatric unit of the Karantina hospital, thanks to private donations and a fierce willpower to serve those abandoned by everyone else. Opened four years prior to mitigate the total failure of the government, it had become the only hope, the only refuge for the destitute, Lebanese and refugees alike. Babies found abandoned and left in the garbage were regularly brought there.

The two doctors, each in their respective hospitals, recount the explosion, describe the damage, and speak of their patients in front of the camera. Each man, at a certain point in his testimony, is choked by sobs and cannot speak. "I just want to cry," says Dr. Sacy, letting his tears fall before the ruins. It completely devastates me to see those two resilient men, habituated to tragedy and pain by the nature of their profession, so consumed by emotion.

The last testimony is that of the mother of the little girl who lost her father. Squeezing the little girl, Gemma, in her arms, she recounts the moment of the explosion and her husband's death in front of her daughter's eyes. She ends by saying, with immense tenderness, that her little girl is very strong, that she didn't shed a single tear.

*A nurse changes his bandage.*
*"Sorry, sweetheart, I know it hurts!"*

*Doctor Sacy.*

*Gemma and her mother.*

## 11

## *The Criminals*

For the Lebanese people, the criminals have always been
the Israelis and the Syrians, the Americans, the Iranians.
After the explosion and the revelation that 2,750 tons of
ammonium nitrate were kept among us for six years, we've
forgotten about those criminals. We've set them aside for
the moment. We are no longer interested in anyone but our
own criminals, the demons that govern us. We are enraged.
We now have just one wish: to see those responsible for this
crime and for the wreckage of the country hanged. A gallows
is built in front of Martyrs' Square. Ropes hang from the
balconies of Beirut, people draw guillotines on the walls of
the city. The guilty are called out, the entire political class,
followed by the financial sector. Those most responsible
are named: "Michel Aoun, Saad Hariri, Hassan Nasrallah,
Nabih Berri, Gebran Bassil, Walid Jumblatt, Suleiman
Frangieh, Samir Geagea, you are the murderers of Beirut,
the assassins of Lebanon, of its model of coexistence and
humanity. You will pay for your crimes. We will not forgive.
We will have vengeance."

These phrases tirelessly repeated on social media and
in the street become my new motto. But only effigies are
hung and burned. I settle for rejoicing that people take
down and trample portraits of Aoun, for celebrating when
people insult him in the crudest fashion, in the most
vulgar terms. Vomit and turd emojis are used to comment
on the speeches of the criminals who govern us, and that

satisfies me. Faced with the extent of the disaster and the despair, these derisory, almost pathetic gestures warm my heart. Which goes to show how little hope I really have that we will be rid of our executioners.

Numerous other leaders, less implicated in the explosion but present on the political scene during the war years, are just as despised and just as responsible for Lebanon's ruin. Their names, heard for too long, inundate everyone's phones. Above all, one of the most booed names for the last several months is that of the governor of the Central Bank, Riad Salameh... #wewillhavevengeance #allmeansall #buildthegallows... Photos depicting the worst political enemies laughing together circulate on social media, highlighting the horrible trick they've played on the Lebanese people. We have no more words potent enough to name them, they are beyond what we can conceive of. Their words and their actions, even after the tragedy, are impossible to believe in the real world. In the worst nightmares or in a horror movie it wouldn't even be imaginable. The days pass, and I have only one desire: for us to be rid of them. I hate them, I want to see them suffer, for their eyes to be gouged out... No... No, what I really want is for them finally to be judged and convicted.

Aoun is so hated that he didn't dare go down to the port or to the most affected neighborhoods. He did not express regrets, apologies, condolences—nothing. Neither him nor any of the other politicians. No regrets and certainly no resignations. The only ministers who went to the devastated neighborhoods are the most insignificant ones, those whose names or faces we barely know. And even so, they are chased out with brooms, literally, while the residents and volunteers, in the absence of any government aid, clean the city streets themselves.

About a month after the explosion, in a very official interview in the presidential palace that was a sad attempt at being dignified, President Aoun appeared in all his infamy, in the most unexpected fashion. I watch the broadcast live. The president's answers are pathetic, outlandish. It's clear that the interviewer, Ricardo Karam—whom I know well— has to make do with it, even if we can see in his face that he is not at all convinced. Suddenly, a question, apparently innocent, almost indulgent, obtains a response that disgusts the Lebanese people. "Mr. President, you have surely followed the events on television, the images broadcast on the news... is there a particular face that has stuck out to you among the victims? Are there certain names that have stayed with you?" The response comes immediately, the president frankly says no, he doesn't really know the names of the victims. Ricardo insists, gives him some ideas. I hold my breath. He will not get any name out of him. Even before the end of the interview, the comments flood social media: "Not even little Alexandra? Not even Elias? He doesn't remember them?" "Not even Sahar?"

*Photos depicting the most bitter political enemies...*

*...laughing together...*

*...are circulated on social media...*

*...highlighting the horrible trick they've played on the Lebanese people.*

*In reality it is these sinister figures…*

*...who must be brought to "justice"...*

*...but there is no justice.*

*Videos of the explosion, watched a hundred times.*
*You can see the yew trees and the roof of Lady Cochrane's villa.*
*Just in front of them, to the right, my parents' building, farther to the right*
*is Centre Sofil, at the very left is the Mar Nkoula church.*

## 12

## *1956 Report on the Port*

An instructive article on the Port of Beirut appeared in the *Revue de géographie de Lyon* in 1956. Here are a few excerpts:

*Beirut, the main port situated on the Mediterranean coast of the Near East, is the point of contact between the countries of the Arab world and the nations of Europe and the Americas. Will the natural vocation of Beirut be impeded by hostile human wills?*

*It's through the relative significance of its hangars that the Port of Beirut acquires its particular physiognomy.*

*The Compagnie du Port delivers to the owners of these goods, upon request, order receipts or warehouse receipts, which allows them to obtain credit for merchandise and also loans abroad, a system that is exceptionally favorable to commerce and speculation. This tendency and this aspect are reinforced by the existence of a free-trade zone which is the port's most distinctive feature.*

*This zone covers a surface area of 106,000 square meters and constitutes on its own a small, very active city. Generally, the merchandise received there is exempt from all customs tax. It can also exit the port without paying any tax on the condition that it is exported by sea.*

*A vibrant commercial center has been created. The sellers can rent premises from the company or locations to construct their own stores. The site is host to various and sometimes curious operations: wool from Australia resold in America, lentils from Turkey shelled and returned to the Indies. Even 50,000 toothbrushes from America spend two years there then leave again for Norway.*

In 1954, 282,000 tons of transit goods passed through this duty-free zone. Of this, 172,000 tons paid no tax.

The rug bazaar is particularly noteworthy, a two-story building in which thirteen Iranian vendors sell 202,500 tons of rugs each year, worth 15 to 16 million Lebanese lira.

A large number of the products received are not immediately exported again but first go through industrial transformations in the factories established in that part of the port. The most notable are a factory for the processing of dried beans, and a factory that manufactures tennis rackets in addition to sausage casings...

If, instead of passing through Beirut, the merchandise reaches Baghdad through Basra, or Tehran through Khorramshahr, after paying taxes at the crossing of the Suez Canal, it must then cross 5,000 additional kilometers for Baghdad and 5,350 kilometers for Tehran. The length of the journey will be increased by twelve to fifteen days and from Basra to Baghdad it must travel another 580 kilometers by train. Given these circumstances, Beirut certainly seems to merit the flattering epithets it often evokes.

Twenty-four shipping lines connect Beirut to all the major ports of the world. Typical port traffic has increased by 20% from 1953 to 1954 and has doubled since 1948. This rise has been accompanied by an increasingly common imbalance between imports and exports.

In 1954, transit goods totaled 403,000 tons, including 40% from port traffic. Of this global figure, Syria represented 171,000 tons, Jordan 106,000 tons, Iraq 61,000 tons—and for all three countries, 84% was in transit through Beirut.

*Nevertheless, the transit of goods through the port represents only a small fraction of Lebanese trade. The previous figures do not take fuel into account. There are two pipelines that terminate in Lebanon: the IPC's (Iraq Petroleum Company) double pipeline in Tripoli, originating in Iraq, and the Aramaco (Tapline), "big inches," originating in Saudi Arabia and terminating in Saida.*

*In recent years there has been a surprising rise in agriculture in Lebanon. The country already has oranges, lemons, apples, onions, and perhaps soon coffee, which people are trying to acclimate to the region. In the industrial sector, hydroelectricity, the country's only source of energy, is valued at 800 kilowatts per hour. After the electricity used for lighting, domestic consumption, irrigation, and the electrification of railroads, 400 million kilowatts/hour remain for industry.*

BEYROUTH LE PORT

*My passion for the Port of Beirut did not begin on August 4.*
*I bought this plate twenty years ago in the Byblos souk.*
*It shows the port in 1969, with its silos under construction.*

All the problems envisaged up til now could be resolved rather easily, because they require only Lebanese intervention or power. This is not the case for projects blamed on neighboring countries.

On the Israeli coast is the Port of Haifa, which is well equipped, and ready, if a solution were brought to the Arab-Israeli conflict, to compete dangerously with the Port of Beirut—an impossible scenario under the present circumstances, but we would be remiss not to mention it.

What will become of the port and the dreams people have for it? Certainly their most laudable quality is that they are modeled narrowly on economic and geographical necessities. These immense hopes aim to turn the Port of Beirut into a vast continental system, the port of five nations.

Nevertheless, there are other imperatives: political, national; desires and jealousies that are far from being to the port's benefit. Beirut will be what its natural circumstances make of it, no doubt, but also what men from all over the Middle and Near East decide to do with it.

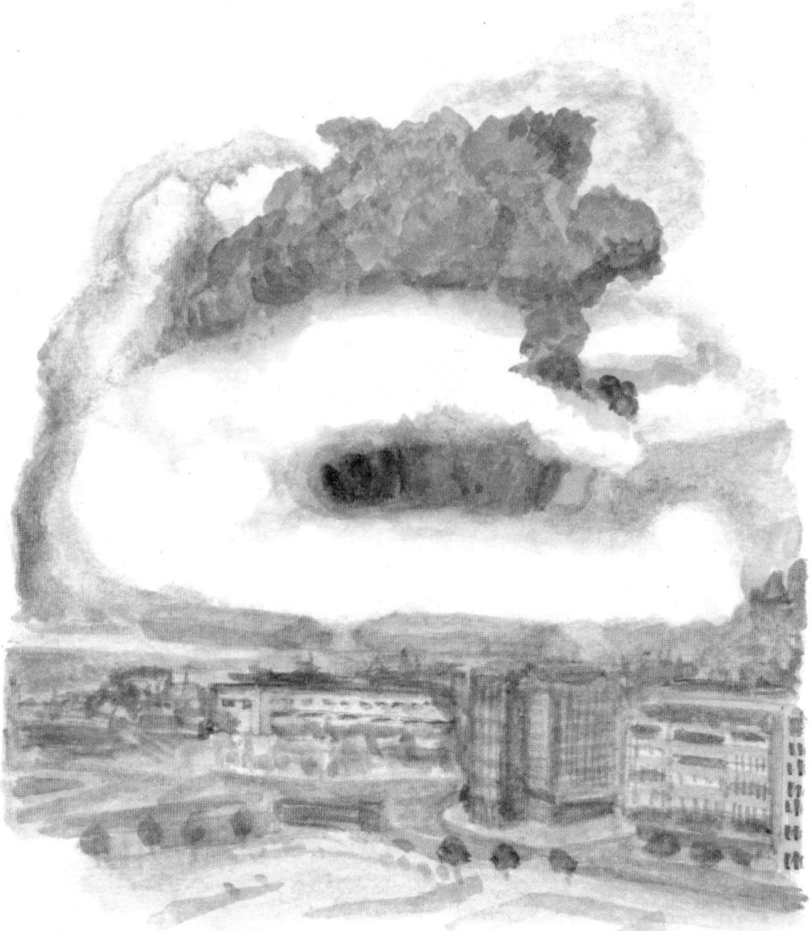

*Poor port…*

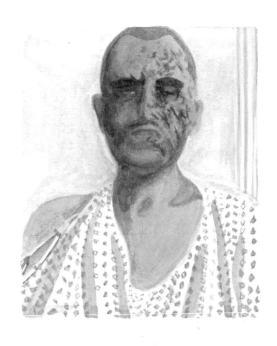

*Mohamed Da'doey was at the port*
*near Hangar 12, in his car, about to return home.*
*He lost partial sight in one eye, is blind in the other, one*
*of his arms is paralyzed and one of his legs amputated.*

*Rony Mecattaf is a psychotherapist.*
*He recounts a recent nightmare. He dreamed of a second*
*explosion during which, this time, he died.*

*A mother on top of her daughter's coffin.*

## 13

## *My Father's Stubbornness*

What happened, after the war? How did we all let everything go to waste? Why did all of society fail, in such a rush to give itself over to superficial pleasures, cheap thrills, frivolity, to "luxury" served on a platter by a political-financial class that was corrupt down to the bone? Why did all of us accept this system that we suspected was bad, without trying to resist, without asking the questions whose answers might have disturbed our comfort, our contentment? Some out of personal interest? Others out of blindness? Others so as not to be sanctimonious, or a killjoy? Out of obliviousness? Because the widespread corruption at every echelon of society seemed to us a quaint and acceptable Lebanese trait? Out of laziness? Because we deemed that we'd had a hard enough time during the fifteen years of war? Suddenly, I have a vision... No, not all of us. We did not all cede so easily. I envision a distant but sharp memory, which I haven't really thought of in twenty-five years: two gendarmes on motorcycles, a car with a fancy license plate, an official ceremony in a neighboring village, the prestigious silhouette of Lebanon's Parliament building in filigree, and in the middle of it all, my father, in a suit and tie.

Before we get to that particular memory, let's start at the beginning of the story.

Just after the war, in 1992, my father ran in the first legislative elections to take place in decades and was elected. The preceding elections had unfurled twenty years prior, three years before the beginning of the war, in 1972. He was twenty-nine years old. After studying law at the Jesuit university in Beirut, then at the Sorbonne, he passed the Beirut bar exam. Passionate about politics, he ran in an election as an independent candidate and lost. For the fifteen years of the war, he had kept himself staunchly removed from all political activity, settling for practicing as a lawyer. In those times, politics went hand in hand with the militia, with weapons, everything that had always horrified him. It didn't align with his idea of how to better serve Lebanon, so he had stepped aside. However, he was often solicited, even intimidated. They offered him weapons to arm his supporters. They promised him high posts in the dominant Christian party, the Phalangists. They ordered him to support this party and its militia. Many of his supporters begged him to accept. Having access to weapons was every Lebanese person's dream in those years. He wouldn't hear of it. He stood strong, despite the criticism and the threats. One night, they decorated the porch of our family house with the party's logo, with a stencil and permanent marker. These intimidations did not make him stray from the course of action he had set for himself: not to participate in the war. Not even in the political sphere.

The years passed, the war ended, we don't really know how, and in the first election, he runs as an independent candidate and is elected deputy speaker and first secretary of Parliament. The man elected speaker that year is none other than Nabih Berri. The two men get along well, Berri is only in his first term. One of the roles of the first secretary is to represent the speaker during official ceremonies when he is not able to be present. My father thus finds himself sometimes at the side of the President of the Republic and the Prime Minister. That their deputy assume this place of honor pleases my father's supporters, his voters, the inhabitants of our region. This duty gives him access to a luxurious official car with a Parliament plate, accompanied by a convoy of a few other cars driven by his partisans, normally Range Rovers, and most importantly, most importantly, the two Lebanese Republic motorcyclists who precede the car and "clear" the road for him, sirens blaring, even when it's perfectly clear already. That is how things are usually done. But my father wants to do things differently. He insists that he has no need for a Parliament car, that his own is sufficient, nor does he need to be escorted by his supporters. He tolerates the two motorcyclists, but asks them not to use their sirens, so as not to bother the other drivers by forcing them to clear the road. But his partisans do not appreciate such discretion. They want for their leader to extol his power, for his convoy to cross the villages of the South, the North, Chouf, Beqaa, and command respect, which is to say with blaring sirens, motorcyclists in full regalia who spread the crowds with their white gloves, the official license plate, the Parliament chauffeur, the shiny car.

They are disappointed. They make it known. He tells them that, like him, they are the first to complain when they have to clear the way for the convoy of a leader they don't know. He doesn't want to do what they criticize others for doing. And if the road is empty, what is the use of blaring the sirens? To announce himself with great fanfare is not his style. No, he will not change his ways. They tell him that he is the only one bothered by it. When a deputy other than him represents Berri, they hear him pass, with his men accompanying him, same thing for the representatives of the President of the Republic or the Prime Minister, everyone struts their stuff when they go from place to place. He will not summon respect if he keeps playing modest. Even his close collaborators insist that he satisfy his supporters from time to time. But my father is stubborn. Verging on hopelessness, one of his most loyal advisors and friends, an important man from our village, begs him: "Next week, you will represent Berri at the archdiocese of Aramoun. In our region. You will travel through your own village and the surrounding villages that make up your fiefdom. We're not asking you to blare your sirens through all of Lebanon, nor that you be accompanied by a procession. But I beg you, when you pass through our village, and the next one, let the motorcyclists turn on their sirens, and the residents, who have known you for so long, will be so proud, you will make them happy." "You're out of your mind," my father cuts him off abruptly. "I'm not going to drive through my own village like a thug." He will tell me with a laugh, once his friend has left: "You see, Lamia, he wants to hear the sirens more than anyone." I didn't dare tell him, ashamed, that I wouldn't have minded either.

My father's obstinacy would end up aggravating everyone, including his most unconditional supporters, including his own family—including me, I admit, although I inherited his distaste for grand displays. I thought that he should make a bit of an effort to please his voters, satisfy their pride at having a leader who flaunts his privileges, even if it went against his principles and his temperament.

*My father in 1972, at the entrance to our house in Qattine.*

Today, at the bottom of the pit we find ourselves in, I see it as an undeniable truth—that the lack of men like my father in politics led to the country's demise. This story of sirens and convoys might seem anecdotal or juvenile. For me it's foundational. The foundation from which to construct a nation. The bare minimum. But my father did not just do the bare minimum. He made a few difficult and courageous decisions, always faithful to his principles. He opposed Hariri's economic policies and refused to vote for the amendment to the Constitution that would allow for the reelection of President Elias Hrawi, backed by the Syrians. He is also one of only five deputies not to have voted for the amendment to the Constitution that would lead to the election of Émile Lahoud, another man supported by the Syrians and made president by Damascus. This resulted in my father losing his deputy seat in the following election. He then joined the movement to force the Syrians to withdraw from Lebanon in 2005, after more than twenty years of occupation. This exploit should have sufficed to guarantee him a victory in the next election, but no. He was defeated by a certain Michel Aoun. Neither the voters, nor anyone else, know yet that Aoun, who has claimed his opposition to the Syrians for more than fifteen years, who waged a deadly (for Lebanon) war against them, in fact entered into a secret agreement with the Syrians prior to the election. It will not be revealed until after he is elected. My father, defeated, retires from politics for good.

August 4 at 6:07 p.m., my father and mother are in our family home in the mountains. My sister tells me that she arrived around 8 p.m., exhausted, traumatized, covered in dust and blood, still trembling, along with my aunt, rattled, barefoot, in a house robe, tattered and bloodstained. She had brought her out of the rubble of her house after traveling on foot through the wrecked neighborhood, crammed with

*My father arriving at a meeting in a coastal village on the last day of the campaign. He will be defeated the next day by Michel Aoun.*

the dead and wounded, to reach her. Also there are my brother, his wife, and their children. Everyone is still in shock. The apartments of my brother and two sisters are destroyed. A few of their friends are dead. They are still stunned and feeble. My father seems unaware that anything has happened, does not participate in the conversation, asks no questions, and watches a documentary on TV about the Kremlin that he had already planned to watch.

LES SILOS CEREALIERS

réalisés par le

CONSEIL EXECUTIF

DES

GRANDS PROJETS

*A brochure someone has just posted on Instagram.*

*Samar is three years old.*

*My sister sent me new photos of my grandmother's house,*
*of a room that was inaccessible after August 4 because of the debris.*
*The small antique pots did not budge...*

*...on their shelves (except one) while the ceiling caved in, and the roof too. At the foot of the intact display case, a heap of plaster, tiles, rafters, planks, glass. Again, the sorcery of objects...*

*Ali Msheik worked at the port, as a day laborer at the silos.*
*On August 4 he was working an extra shift for a few cents more.*
*His wife left to look for him with this ID photo.*
*They have three children.*

The expressway that runs along the port will see many
victims. Cars were thrown several meters before falling back
down, sometimes on their hoods.

# 14

## A Peaceful and Gentle People

Sometimes, I am dazzled by a blinding, painful light. A realization that knocks me down. A puff of anxiety that stops me from breathing, as though I'm about to suffocate, muffled by an overwhelming truth: my whole life, and that of those more or less close to me, has been steeped in violence. Always. I am alarmed by the amplitude and extent of this violence, which has become so familiar that it seems natural to me. That it seems natural to us, to all of us Lebanese people. Why? Why so much violence? Why should it be natural? And yet, I see us as a peaceful and gentle people. An affable people, refined, welcoming, convivial, poets born in a paradisiacal country. Everyone knows this to be true. A peaceful and gentle people whose modern history has been punctuated by tragedy and barbarity. We have accumulated atrocities, even before the beginning of the war and well after it officially ended. Attacks, massacres, bombardments, car bombings. And now this explosion. Beirut has witnessed countless violent deaths. In one of my books, I drew a map of Beirut and marked the places where targeted attacks have taken place. The map is covered in little dots! Why do we live with such violence as thought it were a parent? For so long...

Sometimes, I have the impression that Beirut's violence was born with me, in 1968.

I was born in Beirut in August, seven years before the beginning of the war. Four months later, December 28, 1968, just after 9 p.m., an Israeli commando attacked the

Beirut airport and destroyed thirteen passenger planes from Lebanese airline companies on the ground, which is to say the country's entire civil air fleet. Once the mission was complete, the commando flew away with no issue, while the wreckage of planes burned through the night. Great flames on the tarmac, during the long and sinister black night when Lebanon began to sink. The night of violence.

Two days earlier, two young Palestinian refugees had attacked an El Al airplane at the Athens airport, killing a retired Israeli officer. They were members of the PFLP (Popular Front for the Liberation of Palestine), which takes credit for the attack from Beirut. This is how Israel justifies its attack against Lebanon, holding it responsible for an act committed without its knowledge, outside of its territory and by non-Lebanese people. There is unanimous global condemnation of the Israeli attack, the most firm being that from France. De Gaulle decrees an embargo on weapons destined for Israel, refusing to deliver fifty Mirages that had already been paid for. What happened in Athens was a surprise attack organized by men belonging to a clandestine organization. In Beirut, the operation was launched by a government using its military equipment, notably Super-Frelons and Alouettes manufactured in France, against the civilian facilities of another country.

Here I can't help but point out that the subsequent presidents of France have been cured of such scruples, far less concerned with how military equipment made in France is used.

Lebanon dispatches Fouad Boutros, former Foreign Minister and prominent lawyer, to the UN. Arriving in New York on December 30, he speaks that very night in front of the Security Council, delivering a long speech that will lead three days later to the unanimous condemnation of Israel. The resolution insists on the fact that such premeditated acts of violence threaten the maintenance of peace in the region. Israel is also ordered to reimburse Lebanon for the damages, estimated at 44 million dollars—which Israel will not do.

The airport raid is the first of an endless series of Israeli attacks on Beirut that will take place before, during, and after the war, the majority of them relying on false pretexts. The UN's condemnation will go unheeded and will have no impact on the unbelievable number of violations on Lebanese territory committed by the Israeli air force, 3,000 between 1968 and 1974, sometimes more than once per day, and an average of seven times per day the year before the war. Lacking adequate anti-aircraft defense, the Lebanese skies become the exclusive turf of the Israeli air force. Compared with what followed during the war years and in 2006, most people have forgotten this attack on the Beirut airport. Perhaps some people will remember a certain line that would become famous. After Fouad Boutros's speech in front of the Security Council, Israel's representative tried to justify the attack by presenting Israel as a defenseless victim of Arab aggression. Fouad Boutros addressed the members of the Security Council: "Who will be fooled by Israel's delegate into believing that Israel is the lamb and Lebanon the wolf?"

The next day, December 28, 1967, at dawn, the sun rises, the flames die down, leaving on the tarmac thirteen scorched mounds of wreckage... The first image of the violence.

*December 29, 1968, the sun rises...*

*...over the first images of the violence.*

*Joe Akiki was twenty-three years old.*
*He was working in the silos to pay for his education.*
*On August 4, around three in the afternoon, he reports for duty for a*
*twenty-four-hour shift. Three hours later, he sends a group of friends on*
*WhatsApp a video of the port fire. Then silence. His mother's steadfast belief*
*a few days later, while they are still looking for the bodies, is heartbreaking.*
*She is sure that he is still alive, he is so intelligent and resourceful,*
*he always gets himself out of any situation, he must have found a hole to hide*
*in, he was very familiar with the site, maybe the grain protected him...*

*Ghassan Hasrouti had worked at the port*
*for more than thirty-eight years, also in the silos. Here he is*
*among family, during a celebration in his village.*

## 15

## My Sister on the Phone

Today, my sister tells me: "One of the people at my gym died today after two months in a coma... I saw him every day. We would always pass each other. His session would be at 6 p.m. and mine at 7 p.m. Or the other way around. We would chat a bit. That day, his was at 6 and mine at 7.

"My gym is right across from the silos; 600 meters away.

"Tania, the wife of Hajj, my coach and the gym owner, was outside, filming. Hajj had been in school with me since kindergarten. Hajj was inside. There were a lot of people in the gym... After the explosion, Tania disappeared. Hajj shouts her name, doesn't find her. Everyone searches for her for several minutes, with no luck. Then an arm rises from beneath the debris, far from where she'd been standing. She is 'fine.' Hajj, on the other hand, is wounded and has shards of glass in his eyes. He insists on bringing Tania to the hospital, he thinks she's acting strange. Everyone tells him to leave her there and go to the hospital himself instead. He insists. He starts to go around all the hospitals with her on his moped. He falls several times. She breaks her shoulder and arm. No hospital will take them. After two hours they end up at the Serhal hospital. He's lost a lot of blood and is very weak. As soon as they get there, Tania vomits. Brain scan, brain operation. Hand operation. He has scars all over his face. Another guy from the gym had to get eighty stitches in his neck. I don't know how his carotid artery wasn't severed. Another guy had broken ribs. A girl from the gym is still pulling pieces of glass out of her arm. Her husband went deaf in one ear.

"Krystel was very gravely wounded. She calls her father who's a cardiologist. He is in Ajaltoun. He comes as fast as he can. He finds her under the debris. Gives her CPR. She wakes up for a moment then faints with a sigh. He's a cardiologist, he knows it's a death rattle. He doesn't want to believe it, manages to put her in an ambulance but loses its trail. He looks for her in the emergency rooms of all the Beirut hospitals. He finds her in the American hospital's morgue.

"Kim's sister was thrown so far that she describes having the time to realize she was flying through the room. Kim's baby is safe and sound. She took him from his crib one minute before the explosion to play with its grandfather. The crib is filled with broken glass; it was right in front of the bay window.

"I have to go... I have to take care of my moth problem. I have a crazy moth infestation at my place. Apparently it's happening in all old houses in Beirut right now. When the explosion blasted apart the window and door frames, the moths inside were liberated... Even though I repaired my doors, my windows, and the ceiling, the moths are everywhere now...

"I also need to have my rugs cleaned by an expert. You know they literally shine? I've vacuumed them a hundred times, but they still shine. It's no longer pieces of glass incrusted in it, but the glass dust, which is impossible to get out, and it just shines and shines..."

*Bisan Tibati was seven years old and from Syria.*

*Yehia Hamoui was also Syrian.*

16

# *Who?*

"Why?" "How?" "Who?" "Who?" "Who?" These are the questions in everyone's minds since August 4 at 6:08 p.m.

In 2013, with 2,750 tons of ammonium nitrate on board and a Russian captain, the MV *Rhosus*, a ship registered in Moldova—a country without access to the sea—originating in Georgia and headed for Mozambique, makes a stop in Beirut. It is very old, in a deplorable state. The port authorities forbid it from setting back out to sea. The owner of the ship abandons it, refusing to repair it in the Port of Beirut and to pay the port taxes or his crew. After about a year, it starts to sink. The 2,750 tons are unloaded and stored in Hangar 12, before the ship sinks entirely in the port. Seven years later, as one of the hangar doors is being soldered, a stash of fireworks catches fire and explodes, detonating the ammonium nitrate.

That's the official explanation. But countless questions circle around the arrival of this reserve and why it stayed for seven years in the Port of Beirut. Was the expedition of the *Rhosus*, of its team and its cargo, in fact a fable meant to cover someone's tracks? Was the ammonium nitrate on its way to Hezbollah? Or those three mysterious Syrian businessmen close to Bashar al-Assad? Did the reserve remain in the port out of negligence and incompetence? Or was it intentional? Was Hezbollah using it for something in Syria or elsewhere? Were the three Syrians? Did all 2,750 tons remain at the time of the explosion? Or had the reserve been drawn upon for use in Syria? How many tons exploded in Syria? How many other victims? Who knew that the ammonium nitrate was stashed there? The president? Did everyone know? Many questions and few definitive answers, but one thing is sure: Hezbollah and the politicians in power are undeniably responsible. The rage, the hatred, the anger of the Lebanese people assumed a single target from that point on—the mafioso regime that led us here, that knew.

Whether the Sulta[1] and Hezbollah are criminally responsible for storing the ammonium nitrate in the port is not up for debate, but, over time, another question resurfaces—what was the spark that set the powder on fire? Corruption, incompetence, and negligence are so anchored in power, administration, public services, society, and daily

---

1    Those in power.

life that the accidental origin of the explosion is at first more or less accepted. The soldering story soon proves to be a farce, but even so, the possibility of an accident is not ruled out. Throughout the world people pity Lebanon, help Lebanon, they say: corrupt and irresponsible government. Then: that it was an accident. *The New York* Times even makes a 3D simulation so realistic that there can no longer be any doubt; the story of soldering or an accident, with no semblance of investigation, is entered into History, so to speak. But another theory is in everyone's minds: that of an Israeli "spark." Missile, sabotage, or otherwise. I don't believe there is a single Lebanese who isn't nursing that theory somewhere in their mind. Our long experience with Israeli "politics" regarding Lebanon legitimizes such conjecture.

*On social media, a photo of a man suddenly circulates.*
*We learn that Colonel Joseph Skaff had reported the presence of the*
*ammonium nitrate in the port in 2014, emphasizing the great danger.*
*He had written to the highest authorities to ask that it be safeguarded or*
*destroyed. He was assassinated not long after.*

The videos of the fire, of the explosion, and of the
mushroom cloud are analyzed from every angle, but no
real investigation is ever launched.

## 17

## *Beirut, Nest of Spies*

It seemed crazy to me, the soldering story. This is how I imagine things: one of Mossad's officers comes to Beirut in 2018 on a boat from Athens and passes for a Kurdish, Romanian, or Albanian sailor. The Israelis know that this ammonium nitrate has been languishing in the port for five years. It's just lying there, waiting for them. So they send one of their men. He lingers there for one reason or another, he insinuates himself with the workers on the docks, does favors for the shady officials. I can picture him, he looks like Al Pacino, or maybe Andy Garcia. After a few months, he's a familiar face around the site and friends with everyone, with his thick Bulgarian accent. At the end of July, he unloads a bag of TNT from an Italian cargo ship. Enough to trigger the first explosion. Which detonates the ammonium nitrate.

Or else, another theory: it was one of Mossad's spies. A blonde. She meets one of the port supervisors in a bar in town. Her name is Ingrid, she dreams of being a model, she's from Sweden. She becomes his mistress. After a few weeks, she tells him she'd like to take photos by the port for her lookbook. She begs him to let her pose next to the silos. The day of the shoot, she arrives with the photographer and his assistant, as well as all their equipment. As she poses for photos, they equip the north-west corner of Hangar 12 with explosives and a detonator. On D-day, the photographer and the assistant, emerging from the water like scuba divers, light the fire. Ingrid gives them enough time to swim away and then, from a distance, triggers the first explosion. Which detonates the ammonium nitrate.

If people heard me, they would criticize me for succumbing to conspiracy theories. But for me, life in the Middle East is nothing but conspiracies! I have dinner with a French friend. I amuse him with my imaginings. He says I should offer my services to Netflix. I tell him a few true stories of espionage and Israeli commandos in Lebanon. I have to prove to him that conspiracies really do exist. One of the most famous stories is the assassination of three of the highest-ranking officers of the PLO in Beirut in 1973. The three men, as well as a few other collateral victims, were murdered in their homes, in the middle of the night, by a commando that infiltrated by sea on a raft and landed on a Beirut beach. One of the terrorists who committed the massacre is Ehud Barak, future prime minister of Israel, disguised as a woman, according to the IDF website—and not my overactive imagination. Ahead of the operation, a young woman entered Lebanon pretending to be an American screenwriter who had come to scout a location for a film about the British Orientalist adventurer Lady Hester Stanhope.

I also tell him the story of Mossad's assassination of Ali Hassan Salameh (alias Abu Hassan), the famous "Red Prince," right in the middle of Beirut. The Mossad agent sent to Beirut in 1974 to spy on him sets up shop in a large hotel that Abu Hassan frequents. His orders are to tail him without ever making contact with him. After a few months,

Abu Hassan approaches him while they're both in the hotel gym. The Red Prince suggests a game of squash. They form a genuine friendship. The spy becomes close to him. The Red Prince invites him over to his house, introduces him to his wife, Georgina Rizk, Miss Universe 1971, they share drinks, dinners, gifts. Four years later, it's time to take action. The agent suggests assassination by car bomb.

These two operations are not isolated cases. There are many others. Several Israeli agents, sometimes entire networks, were unmasked in Beirut in the 1950s and 60s, but also in the 2000s and even as recently as 2019. Since the end of the war, it has been primarily Lebanese people employed in telecommunications or high-ranking army officers.

My friend Serge—who is Lebanese—tells me that at the end of the 1970s, a bum with a big beard and a feather cap, Abou el-Rich, was living in a hovel made from cardboard boxes and tires at the foot of their building, between the Marquise ice cream shop and Corner Sport, in the Ras Beirut neighborhood. When his mother let him skateboard in front of the building, Serge enjoyed chatting with him, and Abou el-Rich sometimes helped him with his homework. He spoke several languages fluently including Arabic, French, and English. Serge also heard him speak German with the people from the Goethe Institute, as well as Armenian. People said he was a Lebanese man from Brazil who had squandered his fortune gambling or in business and had gone mad. The residents of the neighborhood liked him a lot. The women brought him cake and bread with labne.

He asked Serge's father for the butts of his Havanas which he sometimes smoked only halfway. In 1982, at the start of the Israeli invasion, Abou el-Rich disappeared, and the people of the neighborhood worried for him. "Poor Abou el-Rich!" Not long after, they learned that he was in fact an Israeli colonel, and saw a photo of him in uniform on the cover of a Lebanese magazine on a tank entering Beirut.

In the first days of the occupation, numerous spies revealed themselves and openly joined the Israelis, while others continued their work in the shadows and would not become known until later. But one thing is sure: every neighborhood of Beirut, sometimes even every street, had a spy of its own in the 1970s. A surgeon from the American hospital tells of a cassette seller who would roam the Hamra neighborhood with a cart back then, music blaring to alert potential buyers. Often he passed under the windows of the hospital, and for years the doctors asked him to turn down the volume, without much success. During the occupation of Beirut by the Israeli army, after three months of blockade and savage bombings, an Israeli officer in uniform came to see the surgeon. It was the cassette seller. He wanted to apologize for the noise, he claimed he was only doing his job. So much arrogance and contempt left the surgeon speechless.

My friend tells me that the current leader of Mossad has just written a book in which he recounts how in 2018 a dozen of his men gained access to Iran's warehouse of nuclear archives in the heart of Tehran, over six consecutive hours broke into thirty-six safes with flamethrowers, and then stole top secret Iranian documents in trucks driven by very well-paid Iranians who had no clue what they were transporting. My jaw drops. Blowing up the Port of Beirut is nothing by comparison. With 2,750 tons of ammonium nitrate already on site, the hardest part is done, it's child's play.

A new video makes the rounds among the Lebanese and
breaks our hearts. It's Sahar, at a Sunday lunch in the mountains.
She dances, she laughs, she kisses her fiancé. Happy times.

*William Azar was thirty-two years old.*

Zeina Chamoun was the mother of three children.
She was at her home in Gemmayzeh on August 4 at 6:07 p.m.

*Youssef Lahoud, a friend of my parents.*
*I was very upset to learn that he had been one of the victims*
*on August 4. His wife Mouna made my wedding dress.*

18

## *The Port, Like the Country*

The port, like the country, is run by gangs. That's what Riad Kobaissi has been saying for years. He is an investigative journalist and activist, one of the pillars of the thawra[2] begun in October 2019. The politicians are mafiosos, the leaders godfathers. The employees and directors, throughout the entire administration and at every level, are not assigned jobs based on their expertise but on their degree of loyalty to the mafia. And based on their religious community according to Lebanon's sectarian political system, with the added bonus that each community is equally corrupt and takes its piece of the pie. Corruption plagues the country. The port is a microcosm of this—the customs authorities in particular. It's a rotten administration where everything is for sale, including explosives. Long before August 4, Riad Kobaissi had already denounced the customs agency and its director, which led to him being sued. He didn't expect as flashy a demonstration of the validity of his accusations as an explosion that would destroy half of Beirut! But it does not change anything; the system is stronger than a quasi-nuclear explosion. Even if the customs director is behind bars for the moment, there was no actual investigation, no defendants, no justice. It's the greatest tragedy of Lebanon, the absence of justice—impunity. The same leaders are still in power five months after the port explosion, thirty years

---

2    Revolution.

*My passion for the Port of Beirut...*
*I bought this Kuwaiti magazine at a bookstore in Hamra a few years ago.*
*The cover photo must have been taken from the top of the silos, which were*
*inaugurated two years prior.*

after the fifteen-year war. This country is led by its worst citizens when it should be the reverse. The most thieving and criminal, who are also the most incompetent. And yet, everyone knows that Lebanon is not lacking in talent.

A quotation by Robert Fisk has circulated endlessly on social media since that summer: "So here is one of the most educated nations in the region with the most talented and courageous—and generous and kindliest—of peoples, blessed by snows and mountains and Roman ruins and the finest food and the greatest intellect and a history of millennia. And yet it cannot run its currency, supply its electric power, cure its sick or protect its people."

Yes, they exist, these talented, courageous, generous citizens. These men and women who, right now in Lebanon, are fighting to reconstruct the city, to care and feed, to inform and resist.

*"...protect its people..."*

19

## *Thawra, Birth of a Nation*

The mutual aid in Beirut during the weeks after the explosion is as spectacular as the blast itself. Countless NGOs, big and small, arrive on the scene. They replace the failing and criminal government. Certain among them, created during the war in the 1980s, have become quite robust in domains as diverse as health, construction, education, food banks intended to help disadvantaged Lebanese people and refugees alike. They have literally become a state within the state, and in fact the government sometimes subcontracts them for projects it is unable to complete successfully, such as the construction of schools or prisons. After August 4, thousands of volunteers join them. In forty-eight hours, six thousand people answer the call of Offrejoie, one of the most structured organizations. These associations that date from the war have been joined by a number of newcomers, many born out of the October 2019 revolution, and by young Instagram activists who use their influence to build rapid and efficient solidarity networks. Regular citizens have taken matters into their own hands. They are the real Lebanon. A plea is broadcast over every network: Send donations from governments and international or private organizations directly to the people on the ground. Please do not give anything to the corrupt government.

In the first days after the explosion, the only sound that runs through the dazed city is the delicate whispering of glass debris, the squeaking of shards being swept away everywhere.

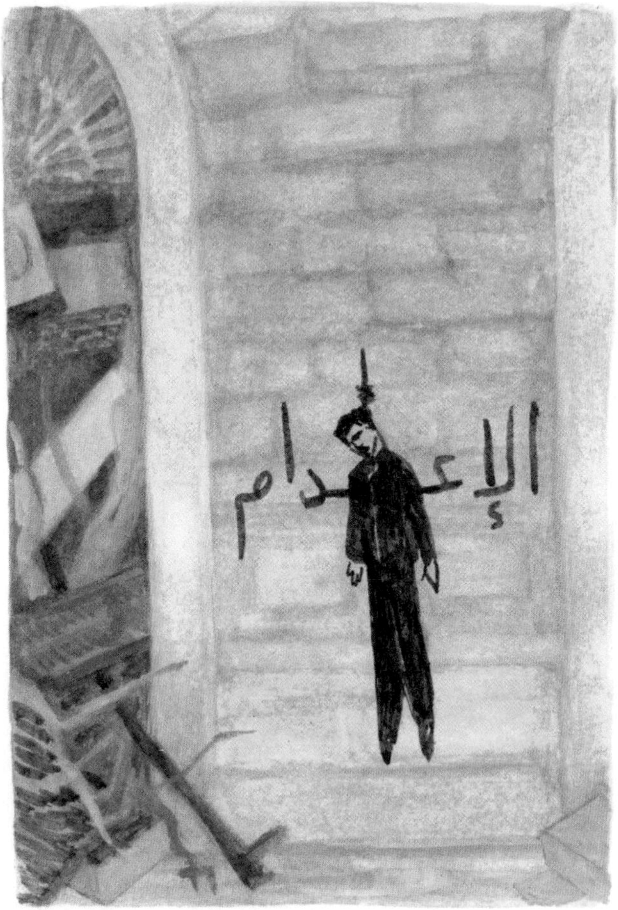
الإعدام

*Not far from the port.*

The inhabitants of Beirut have cleared the grounds and cleaned their city themselves. No aid from the city, the state, or the army; quite the contrary. The people who aren't dead or wounded, or only slightly hurt, grabbed shovels, brooms, brushes, and tidied the street. They removed the debris and the broken windows, helped the old, sick, and wounded leave their houses or apartments, then repaired the most urgent things, roofs, doors, windows. From the first day, even in a state of emergency, they sifted through it all, because everything, or nearly everything, is salvageable in a country in crisis. The glass, the wood, the moldings, the iron, the tiles. They did things right. For the old traditional houses, this work is particularly important because such homes must be rebuilt from the same elements. These volunteers are the ones who reconstructed the nation. The volunteers, versus the vultures.

Glued to my phone, I scrutinize the slightest sign, the smallest action that could signal the beginning of the end for those crooks who have led Lebanon to its demise—in vain. Days pass and nothing happens. Except for all the new, endless horrors. Political, economical, or related to security. My poor country is in agony, my city is on its knees, and these monsters are still cracking the whip. Worse than before. They are more thieving, more dishonest, more criminal. Now they fire live bullets at protestors, jail them, bring them in front of the military tribune. Fear reigns now, as in the worst of totalitarian countries. Yes, in Lebanon, country of free expression, refuge for the revolutionary silenced or imprisoned in any other Arab country, the people have been handed over to the Sulta.

*"They are the real Lebanon..."*

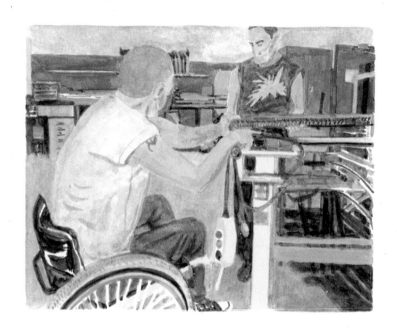

*Crutches, wheelchairs, and walkers are manufactured in the workshop
of arcenciel, one of the oldest NGOs in Lebanon.*

*They are more competent and useful to society*
*than any minister or banker.*

*Repairing the roofs of Beirut.*

And yet, the thawra, begun October 17, 2019, continues. There's no longer a big crowd. People are tired, emptied, disillusioned. People fear repression by the Lebanese Internal Security Forces and the army and intimidation by Amal[3] and Hezbollah's men. But some citizens still take to the streets every day. Several times per day. They stand strong on every front, every topic, don't let anything go. Vigilant. They are Lebanon's only chance, there is no other. Them, and those who care, who feed, who clean. Sometimes, maybe often, they are the same people. They are the ones who prioritize the country and society ahead of their own interest or that of their sectarian community. Lebanon is not a country where that comes naturally. These men and women are heroes, they are courageous and fight in hope of finally constructing a nation. That also does not come naturally. The word "hope." What madness.

For a year now, I've been following several leaders of the revolution on Instragram, checking for updates almost every hour, glancing only distractedly at the other accounts I follow. There's the loudmouthed activist and the social activist, the pro-bono lawyer, the militant journalist, the active actor... There are collectives that get things done, people on site, people who circulate information and analysis, who manage the operations... There is also the incredible ThawraMap, which, thanks to a vast anonymous and effective network, tracks politicians in real time, and alerts thousands of followers to their presence in this restaurant or that mall so they can show up and harass their prey until they leave or at

---

3    Amal: Shiite party allied with Hezbollah.

*Many protestors will lose an eye...*

least bombard them with shame, assuming the politician in question has even a modicum of self-respect.

And then there are the accounts that make us laugh. Ammounz, for example, the most foul-mouthed girl you could imagine, who makes short videos in which she

*Some Instagram accounts of the thawra.*

addresses the president or the prime minister in extremely informal Arabic. And FarixTube—Farid Hobeiche—whose subtle and hilarious videos describe the daily life of the Lebanese in the shitshow that is their country.

Someone has just posted a photo from a protest last November, the Eden Bay protest, with a nostalgic caption. Suddenly, I shudder. That protest—I was there. The distance

*The sharp-tongued Ammounz.*

*Thank goodness for Farid Hobeiche, also known as FarixTube.*

"His Excellency the Murderer."

that separates me now, always on the verge of tears, crying several times a day, from that moment of euphoria and wild hope is so dizzying it makes my head spin. I am teleported back to November, I relive my thirty days in the thawra as if I were there, as if I could turn back time then stop it and resume the course of events when everything was still possible.

*I took this photo on rue Hamra in November 2019.*

## 20

## *October 17*

I arrive in Beirut on October 31, 2019. A revolt, already being called a revolution, broke out in Lebanon on October 17. In the half-empty plane I am feverish, excited by the unknown of the days to come. A sentiment I know well, one I've felt for a long time, similar to the feeling I would get upon my return to Lebanon during the two last years of the war, when I was a student in Paris. Those numerous returns were full of the promise of intense, dangerous, frightening moments, everything I dreaded but that also made me feel alive.

I drop off my suitcase then head downtown on foot, to Riad el-Solh Square and Martyrs' Square, where everything is happening. For a few days, the protests block the streets all over Lebanon, starting with the Ring. For someone who lived through the war, the closing of the Ring is familiar. Familiar and funereal. It remained closed for fifteen years and, in the beginning, those who tried to take it anyway had little chance of arriving at their destination, coming under fire from snipers on one side or the other, which is why it was called the Ring of Death. Today it's nothing like that, because this isn't the war, but the revolution. And it's a revolution that has already earned a reputation for being peaceful, congenial, festive, of the people... But I can't help it, this feeling of déjà-vu won't ever leave me again, and memories of the war will come rushing back at various moments in the following weeks. On the ground, my apprehensions disappear for a little while. I join the party, thrilled. Since its controversial reconstruction, downtown Beirut had become a proper neighborhood, "chic", expensive, inaccessible to the working class, so different from what it had been for centuries, a place of conviviality, of social and community intermingling. Since October 17, it has been taken over once more by a mixed crowd, not unlike the one that forged the reputation of pre-war Beirut. Everywhere there are street peddlers selling grilled corn, knafeh cooked over wood fire, brochettes, kaak, I hadn't seen that in this neighborhood since 1975! There are families with children, bands of young people, elderly men and women, artists, intellectuals, the unemployed, rich, poor... Some people gather around an improvised platform, others sing popular songs with the lyrics changed to mock our despised leaders, others chant funny and impertinent slogans.

The soldiers who stand guard around that gigantic zone are phlegmatic. They don't seem perturbed by the demands for the fall of those in power. Right in the beating heart of the protest, they lean on security barriers or against cars in lascivious, even voluptuous poses, holding a cigarette or a sandwich. They look like they're on their day off, at a nice picnic by the sea or a wedding in a mountain village, waiting for the bride to arrive... You can see on their faces that they wish they could join the celebration or the fury of the crowd.

How things will change! These are the same men who now attack protestors with extreme violence. And, more recently, with live bullets.

At these good-natured protests, I could have
crossed paths with little Alexandra and her parents.
This photo was taken at Azarieh and breaks my heart.

*I love this banner from before August 4.*
*It's fun, untranslatable, but something along the lines of:*
*We've been getting screwed for 40 years.*
*Now it's your turn. Please, it's the least we can do.*
*Anything for you. The slogan on her T-shirt reads: Enough is Enough.*
*After August 4, only rage is possible.*

When the people are hungry they eat their leaders.
Gebran Bassil son of a bitch.
Leave. Get the fuck out.
Down with the rule of the banks.
Pay back the stolen money.
Michel Aoun is dead.
It's the heart of Beirut, not Solidere[4].
A Lebanese feature film.

---

4     Solidere (The Lebanese Company for the Development &
Reconstruction of Beirut Central District) is a real estate company created
to redevelop Beirut city center after the end of the Lebanese Civil War.
Controversial for its use of forced evictions and property exploitation,
Solidere has come to represent for many the political and economic
corruption in Lebanon.

*Riad el-Solh Square. At the bottom left, the Grand Serail.*
*Between the two buildings, the beginning of Banks Street.*
*To the right, the entrance of the street leading to Parliament.*

Slogans cover the walls. All the leaders are lambasted there. *Kellon ya3ne kellon.* "All means all" is the rallying cry of this revolution. They are insulted in the most vulgar terms. All called thieves. All demanded to be held accountable. People want the stolen money. I take photos of every slogan. An archivist. I am full of hope. I enter the Grand Théâtre (where Umm Kulthum sang in the 1930s), dazzled by this ruin which has been off limits since the end of the war. Then I enter "the egg," the carcass of a cinema in futurist architecture where today people hold debates open to everyone. The revolution has taken over these confiscated places, each symbolic. I am fascinated by the masters of ghazal, the very Lebanese art of rhetoric, which is performed, similarly to slam poetry, through delicious verbal jousts. Two or three virtuosos entertain the crowd. In their verses they lambast politicians with wit, audacity, and insolence. The award for the most despised man of the Republic goes to Gebran Bassil, the president's son-in-law. From time to time, people launch into the national anthem, and suddenly tears spring to my eyes. Emotional, it takes me a few seconds to get a hold of myself and passionately join into the chorus.

The next day is the Eden Bay protest. The procession moves along the Corniche and heads for the five-star hotel complex constructed completely illegally on a beach in south Beirut, Ramlet el-Baida, a place where pouring concrete is forbidden. This fraudulent privatization of the Lebanese coast was made possible for one simple reason: the owner of the hotel, Wissam Achour, is close to Hariri and Berri. There are even rumors that it's a shell corporation... People chant joyous, sophisticated slogans, but the message is clear and can be summed up as follows: "Hariri, thief, Berri, thief, Achour, thief, give back the coast and the lands stolen from the Lebanese people."

When we near the entrance of Eden Bay, we cannot go another step farther. Soldiers block the way. The goal of the protest is not to clash with the army, so we stop, and the protest continues in place. Eventually the excitement dies down and we decide it's time to go home. The end of the procession starts to filter out. They ask us to move aside to let through a blocked car that's carrying a sick person. As per usual, we step aside only half believing the story. And of course, it's not one car that bursts through the guard of

*At the end of Ramlet el-Baida, on the outer wall
of Eden Bay, the word "thawra."*

honor formed by the crowd split in two, but ten, fifteen, twenty cars, and that's when something magical happens, something which transforms the half-extinguished protest into an extraordinary spectacle: two young men yell at every car that rushes through the crowd: "If you're with the revolution, honk your horns!" A feverish clamor of horns mixes with the applause and chants of the people, stirring up the procession in an unexpected way. The vivid memory of that moment of euphoria pains me today. That moment when we were about to change the world soon gave way to the worst of nightmares.

To go back to the house, my sister and I make our way through Beirut's inland neighborhoods. Jnah, Cola, Msaytbeh, Mar Elias, Dar el-Fatwa... Suddenly, in the dim side streets of a residential neighborhood, a vague background noise, nearby, regular, resounding, reaches through the open windows of the car. Street after street, the sound does not fade, it accompanies us, a small racket, with nuance and variation... "It's pots!" my sister cries. That morning, we had seen a call on Instagram to bang on pots for five minutes at 8 p.m. as a sign of protest. We had liked the idea but thought it was too short notice for people to get the message, and then we had forgotten about it the rest of the day. It had worked! On every street, three or four women on their balconies, no more, but it was enough! Disappointed at not being home to participate, I stick my arm out the car window and pound on the body of the car, and other drivers soon follow suit. Then we learn that this act of resistance will be repeated every day at 8 p.m. I am delighted, I promise myself that I will be home for it the next day. "You're crazy!" my sister says to me, "You can't do that in your neighborhood! There's an Amal presence on your street! They're all over your area."

*The entrance to the Électricité du Liban building, 550 meters from the silos, after August 4.*

I tell myself that she's overreacting, that this isn't the war anymore. Those militias watch TV all day long, smoking and drinking coffee on the sidewalk. They seem harmless, maybe even nice. And then suddenly, that nagging question: What if, in the end, nothing has changed since the war? If everything suddenly reverted? All it would take is a spark...

The next day at 8 p.m., I'm on my balcony. I'm forced to admit that my sister was right, no one, absolutely no one is banging on a pot on my street, nor in the adjacent streets.

Listening closely, I can hear the rumble coming from the surrounding neighborhoods.

In the following days the targeted forms of protest multiply. In front of the courthouse, in front of the Banque du Liban... Sunday at 7 p.m., the crowd meets in front of the Électricité du Liban building, the national temple of corruption. There are huge throngs of protestors. As usual, there are also people on balconies overlooking the crowd. And also as usual, the protestors look up at these passive spectators and yell a mocking slogan that has become a ritual: "Hey you on your balconies, come down and be revolutionaries!" Tonight, there are entire families up there, but no one budges. There are speeches. As is typical in these large protests, we sing a famous ballad by Marcel Khalife, "Ya Bahriyé." Suddenly, an incredible racket surpasses the clamor of the protest. The pots! It's eight o'clock and we've forgotten all about it. But the people on their balconies haven't forgotten, and they are not shy! For five minutes they bang as loudly as they can, from all the surrounding buildings, doubling the roar of the crowd who are thrilled by this surprise. It's fantastic! The memory of this night pains me. What a waste!

*Banque du Liban, rue Hamra.*

*The apocalypse...*

## 21

# *Things Take a Turn*

November 12, 2019, things suddenly start to accelerate. A man is beaten in front of his wife and twelve-year-old son at a protest in Jiyeh. Of course, the scene is filmed on cellphones and circulates around the country over WhatsApp at lightning speed. Everyone in Lebanon heard the lacerating screams of Alaa Abou Fakhr's wife and saw the sight of his blood. Fear and anger are in everyone's minds, the fear that things will spiral out of control definitively. The killer is a soldier who is arrested. The victim, immediately labeled a martyr, is Druze and a member of the Progressive Socialist Party, whose leader is Walid Jumblatt, as un-socialist as possible and also the Druze leader. As soon as the news breaks, Jumblatt visits the family of the deceased, despite being one of the politicians most targeted by the revolution. Firmly, he calls on the gathering of angry men surrounding him to renounce vengeance and wait for justice to do its work. He tells them not to lead the country into a deadly spiral. His address to the martyr's loved ones and to the members of his party is also filmed on phones and makes its way around Lebanon. This shows me that, despite several weeks of uprising against the political establishment and despite the fact that Walid Jumblatt is the personification of it, his power over the protestors and his community has in reality not changed. I am enraged. No, absolutely nothing has changed... The president will speak on television that very night.

Before the broadcast has even finished, people are in the streets. For a week the revolution has been at something of a standstill, has receded into a morose routine, and the death of Alaa Abou Fakhr added a dose of fear and discouragement... Now, with just a few sentences, Aoun has

*On every phone, the video of the murder, and also this*
*photo of Alaa with his children.*

unleashed a storm against himself. Against him personally. We forget the others, all the others, now it's his head we want. In Beirut, the first to take to the streets do not go downtown as usual; instead they go directly to *shut down* the Ring. My sister and I are among them. The streets are blocked in all the cities of Lebanon. Everywhere people are revolted by the president's speech. We insult him now without holding back, the crowd is in a frenzy. New slogans surge, with Aoun the target of them all. There's an amazing young woman with a megaphone. She yells improvised slogans and the crowd around her repeats each one. This goes on for a while, each time a new phrase. Most of the people around her are men. Led by this tiny woman, they take up her incantations with fury.

The next day, the funeral of Alaa Abou Fakhr, called the "martyr of the revolution," brings life to all of Lebanon. Everywhere people light candles, paint his portrait on walls, write messages of support to his family. His wife Lara, a woman of character, cries over his open casket covered in mountains of flowers. Leaning over the peaceful face of her husband, caressing it from time to time, she addresses him as though they were alone, but screaming as loudly as she can. She wants the entire world to know her love and her pain, to hear her fierce declarations of love and intimate reproaches, aggravated and poignant: "What am I going to do now? Who will tell me if my mujaddara needs salt? Who will prepare the hookah for me every night?" The bells toll in homage to the martyr, despite the fact that he's Druze.

Just two days later, a dramatic turn of events brings me hope again. A new Prime Minister is suddenly named. But my optimism only lasts a matter of minutes, the time it takes to read about him online... Is this a joke? Not only is the man over seventy-five years old, but he has been involved in countless business dealings. The typical profile of the shady politician denounced by the protests since the beginning of the revolution. All the streets are blocked again. Hordes of people on social media are quick to mock the man and

*Lara and Alaa.*

those who appointed him. They really outdo themselves! His Wikipedia page is edited within the hour by pranksters who list all of his misdeeds. The man is skewered before he is even officially appointed, we have a good laugh, but above all we want to cry. We have no idea that just one year later, Hariri will be Prime Minister again. It's a curse.

I print out a poster and paste it to the walls of the city. It's a drawing of a woman screaming, taken from my book *Ô nuit Ô mes yeux*, with the word *thawra* at the bottom. In my books, especially in *Ma très grande mélancolie arabe*, I've reproduced many political, partisan, or activist posters, which made history in the Middle East and formerly covered the walls of Beirut. I am very proud to be a part of this history in my own way. To bring things full circle, I take a photograph of myself on a side street of the corniche, in front of a poster from the 1970s that has been recirculated recently, depicting Gamal Abdel Nasser. I had drawn this poster in my book *Bye Bye Babylon*.

End of November, the Beirut Bar Association has its presidential election. The stakes are high. A candidate of the revolution runs. Melhem Khalaf beats a candidate supported by all the Lebanese political parties by a large number of votes. At the announcement of his victory, the hall filled with lawyers explodes, several groups of jubilant lawyers brandish their fists and chant, "thawra, thawra," revolution, revolution, as though they were on Martyrs' Square. The new president, charismatic and impressive, has been at the protests since the beginning. He embodies the ideas of immense progress and hope. Founder in the 1980s of the humanitarian organization Offrejoie, one of the

The Bar Association of Beirut,
"Mother of Laws"

*In Antiquity, the Beirut school of law shone over the Mediterranean...*
*Today, in Lebanon, the word "justice" no longer exists.*

most important and active organizations in Lebanon in every community, he is a fervent promoter of Muslim-Christian understanding, very active in numerous fights for greater social justice, tolerance, and human rights. His trajectory is not the standard one, which begs the question: is the tide beginning to turn?

Alas, no! In the weeks that follow, Lebanon deteriorates. The economic crisis worsens with each day. Some people, desperate, no longer have the strength to protest, only to kill themselves. The ISF assault protestors as brutally as Amal forces or the Parliament militia. The Coronavirus pandemic isolates people at home... I am enraged at the idea of the quashed revolution. I want so badly to believe that it was not a parenthesis that has closed once more. I am furious at my powerlessness.

*Majida Kassab was at her mother's bedside at the orthodox hospital
on August 4 at 6:07 p.m.
Her mother survived but Majida lost her life.*

*Days of rage on the walls of Beirut.*

*Days of fury.*

Today, more than a year after the beginning of the thawra, nearly six months after the port explosion, I have no more hope. The situation is beyond tragic, on every level. Coronavirus rages, the hospitals are full, even utilizing their parking lots, their staff are completely exhausted, Hariri is back and as incapable as before, Hezbollah is still present, Aoun and the rest are still there, the thawra is savagely repressed, the economic situation is catastrophic, several assassinations have taken place, visibly linked to the port explosion, whose investigation is a great farce. The Lebanese people are distraught, hopeless. Israeli fighter jets fly over Lebanon, including Beirut, with a dreadful racket several times per day, very low in the sky, terrorizing an already traumatized population.

We will not overcome August 4. Not without a miracle. That is our only chance.

A Lebanese friend who lives in Paris told me a few days ago that she stood in front of the half-open door of her seven-year-old daughter's bedroom and glimpsed her on her knees next to her bed, hands clasped, in the middle of praying: "And please, God, help Lebanon." "I had goosebumps," my friend tells me, "I saw myself at her age, in the same pose, saying the same words. It will never end, it's a curse!"

Suddenly, a miracle. The victory of independent and secular candidates of the thawra in the student elections, in all the universities of Lebanon, is a real reason to rejoice. It's an historical win. Until now, the universities had always been infiltrated by the parties. It would have been unthinkable for an independent candidate to come out on top. Now, the parties have been dismissed, the thawra continues!

For several weeks now, I've been obsessed by knowing the exact date the silos were constructed. Finally, I have the information before my eyes: first stone, September 1968. So I was not only born with the violence, but also with the silos. Inauguration, August 1970. Fifty years ago.

The port silos so staunchly resisted the explosion that they saved a part of Beirut from destruction and saved many lives. The neighborhoods located to the south-west of the silos, opposite from hangar 12, were relatively spared. All the experts agree that if it hadn't been contained by the silos, the explosion blast would have caused much more damage to the west, resulting in many more victims.

I can't help but think of the resistance of Cinema Rivoli and its large "ORIENT" sign. Its resistance to another kind of explosion. This massive stone building was located at the end of Martyrs' Square, on the coast. It valiantly resisted fifteen years of war with barely a scratch. When Beirut was reconstructed by Solidere, today largely recognized as a huge, corrupt property development organization, the Art Deco aesthetic of this mythical cinema offended the Saudi sensibility of Rafic Hariri and his delusions of grandeur. Instead, he wanted to build "an avenue wider than the Champs-Élysées." So they blew up that building, a symbol of pre-war Lebanon and certainly the most photographed and reproduced building besides the Baalbek temples. They will have to try four times before the cinema is brought down, increasing the amount of explosives each time. The Rivoli is finally pulverized in a gigantic implosion, defeated by the new game masters, then razed.

Since August 4, the silos have been photographed from a single angle, the side of the explosion. They are a gaunt, disfigured, mutilated, monstrous carcass.

Seen from the other side, the west side, they are still very white and very straight, mostly intact. I see it as another symbol, that all is not lost. All the more so because the west side is the side that catches the light. The light that comes from the sea. The light of the setting sun.

*Paris, January 20, 2021*

I finished this book a few days ago.
But this morning, a short video brought tears to my eyes.
I have to add one last drawing.
It's from Sahar's birthday, exactly one year ago, at the Karantina fire station.

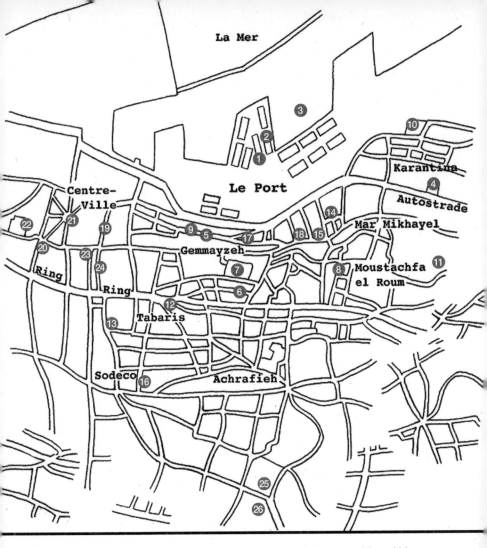

La Mer

Le Port

Karantina

Centre-Ville

Autostrade

Mar Mikhayel

Gemmayzeh

Moustachfa el Roum

Ring

Ring

Tabaris

Sodeco

Achrafieh

1  The silos
2  Hangar 12
3  The third basin
4  The fire station
5  My grandmother's house
6  My parents' apartment
7  Lady Cochrane's villa
8  The orthodox hospital
9  The Wardieh hospital/
   Rosary Sisters Hospital

10  The Karantina hospital
11  The Geitawi hospital
12  My sister Nayla's house
13  My sister Youmna's office
14  The Skyline building
15  The East Village building
16  The Sama Beirut building
17  Nayla's gym
18  EDL (Électricité du Liban)

19  Martyrs' Monument
20  Riad el-Solh Square
21  Parliament
22  Grand Serail
23  Grand Théâtre
24  The Egg
25  Hôtel-Dieu
26  Palais de Justice

The illustrations in this book were based primarily on photos circulated on social media, especially Instagram. Their origins are thus often unknown, as is also the case for the stories and information relayed in these posts.

Here I have tried to list as many accounts as possible that served as my sources:
@august4memorial @lebanontimes @livelovebeirut @lorientlejour @gregorybuchakjian @daliakhamissy @myriamboulos @arcenciel @beirutheritageinitiative @bakalianmills @megaphonenews @daleelthawra @thawramap @ginoraidy @ayahbdeir @leb.historian @ammounz @farixtube

The photo of Pamela Zeinoun and the three babies was taken by Bilal Jawish.

The photos and testimonies from the chapter "Sacy and Noun" come from the reportage *In the Chaos of Hospitals* by Sylvain Lepetit, Chloé Domat, Wissam Charaf, and Sophie Guignon.

The photos and testimonies from the chapter "The Orthodox Hospital" come from *Heroes Wear Scrubs*, a film by Zeina Farah.

To support Lebanon:
offrejoie.org
arcenciel.org
redcross.org.lb
beirutheritageinitiative.com
assamehbb.org (Doctor Sacy's organization)

The excerpts from Chapter 12 were taken from an article in *Revue de géographie de Lyon*: "The Port of Beirut," by Jean Laugenie, 1956.

A few pages from an earlier version of this book appeared in *M le Monde* and *Vanity Fair* at the time of the Beirut explosion and the thawra.